# CHERISHED EXPERIENCES

## FROM THE WRITINGS OF

# PRESIDENT DAVID O. McKAY

# CHERISHED EXPERIENCES
## FROM THE WRITINGS OF
# PRESIDENT
# DAVID O. McKAY

*Compiled by Clare Middlemiss*

Published by
Deseret Book Co.
Salt Lake City, Utah
1976

Library of Congress Catalog Card No. 76-5178
ISBN 0-87747-030-8

Printed in the United States of America

# Contents

SECTION V: Inspirational Stories for Youth

# Preface

*Great men taken up in any way, are profitable company. We cannot look however imperfectly upon a great man without gaining something by him. He is the living light-fountain, which it is good and pleasant to be near. The light which enlightens, which has enlightened the world; and this not as a kindled lamp only, but rather as a natural luminary shining by the gift of heaven; a flowing light-fountain, as I say, of native original insight, of manhood and heroic nobleness; in whose radiance all souls feel that it is well with them.* (*Thomas Carlyle*)

Beginning in the spring of 1935, it was my great privilege to serve as secretary to President David O. McKay. During this long and close association, I was singularly blessed. I was in the presence of a man of God, a great and inspired leader; a "living light-fountain"; a man who believed in the sacredness and dignity of the individual, and whose whole purpose in life was to bring happiness and salvation to his fellowmen.

In gathering and preserving in scrapbooks a vast store of clippings, speeches, editorials, special letters, and notes concerning the activities of President McKay, I have been profoundly impressed with the magnitude of the work accomplished and the service rendered by him throughout seventy-two years, beginning with his call to his first mission as a young man in 1897 and continuing to the end of his life as President of the Church in 1970.

During his presidency of the Church and before, President McKay interviewed and welcomed thousands of persons, members and nonmembers alike; and as he told them of the gospel, they felt his sincerity and the warmth of his personality. He received the humble and the great; children and young people were especially welcomed. Among the important and distinguished persons who called upon him or whom he met in his world travels were Queen Juliana of the Netherlands, President Juho K. Paasikivi of Finland, President Juan Peron of Argentina, Crown Prince Tungi of Tonga, King Tamasese, King Malietoa, and King Mata'afa of Samoa, President and Mrs. Harry S. Truman, President Dwight D. Eisenhower, President John F. Kennedy (whom he met first as a young senator), President and Mrs. Lyndon B. Johnson, and President and Mrs. Richard M. Nixon. President McKay was invited to the White House on several occasions by some of these Presidents. He was also visited by United States Vice Presidents, presidential candidates, foreign ambassadors and consuls, bankers, educators, economists, medical men, journalists, labor leaders— indeed, men from all walks of life. Many interesting and fascinating stories could be told of the interviews and impressions made during these visits.

During his presidency of the Church, President and Sister McKay traveled approximately 150,000 miles by air throughout the United States, England, Germany, Austria, Switzerland, Scandinavia, Holland, France, South Africa, Brazil, Argentina, Uruguay, Chile, Guatemala, Mexico, Australia, New Zealand, and the islands of the South Pacific. It would be impossible to estimate the number of miles he traveled also during the years he served as an apostle and as a counselor in the First Presidency. On his world tour of missions in 1921, he traveled 62,500 miles by land and sea at a time when the comforts of travel that now exist were unknown.

John Foster Dulles, United States Secretary of State, in a personal letter to President McKay dated March 31, 1954, commended President and Sister McKay for their "notable service to the United States in their travels as unofficial ambassadors of good will." Among the tributes paid to him was this one: "He is a man who seems to feel the heartbeat of the world. With a dedicated sense of vision he has endeavored with unique success to build everywhere a community of good will, sympathetic tolerance, and creative humanitarianism." (Dr. Henry Beattyon.) Many other tributes came from distinguished men and women throughout the world who were impressed with his dignity, outstanding personality, and spirituality.

President McKay was one of the great missionaries of the Church. No one person had had so much to do with the missionary work of the Church as had he at the time of his death in January 1970. He stated, upon his arrival in Papeete, Tahiti, January 18, 1955: "Sister McKay and I are flying by land and sea, telling the story, first, of the glories of the restored gospel, and, second, assuring our members of the Church in all lands that we are all one—members of the divine church—children of our Father in heaven."

In 1934, when David O. McKay became a member of the First Presidency, President Heber J. Grant appointed him chairman of the Church Missionary Committee. His whole heart and soul were devoted to this special assignment. In addition to this and other duties associated with the office of the First Presidency, he delivered hundreds of major addresses and performed untold numbers of marriages for young people in the temple. Two file drawers are full of copies of sermons he delivered at the last rites held for General Authorities, stake presidents, bishops, friends, relatives, and many others.

He was called as an apostle in April 1906 by President Joseph F. Smith and served in the Council of the Twelve for forty-five years. Nearly seventeen years of that time he served as second counselor in the First Presidency, first to President Heber J. Grant from 1934 to 1945, and then to President George Albert Smith until 1951.

At the age of 76, he was sustained as Prophet, Seer, and Revelator of the Church at a solemn assembly in the Salt Lake Tabernacle on Monday, April 9, 1951. With humility and great spirituality, he acknowledged the greatest honor and responsibility that could come to him in the Church, declaring, "No one can preside over this church without first being in tune with the Head of the Church, our Lord and Savior Jesus Christ. He is our Head. This is his church. Without his divine guidance and constant inspiration, we cannot succeed. With his guidance, with his inspiration, we cannot fail!" Then he added: "Next to that, as a sustaining, potent power, come the confidence, faith, prayers, and united support of the members of the Church."

In May 1952, at age 78, President McKay, in company with Sister McKay, again took up his world travels. He delivered hundreds of addresses and dedicated many church buildings. He dedicated the Swiss Temple, the first temple to be erected in Europe, on September 11, 1955. Two more temples erected in foreign lands were also dedicated by President McKay—the New Zealand Temple at Hamilton, New Zealand, on April 20, 1958, and the London Temple in Great Britain on September 7, 1958. He also dedicated two temples in the United States—the Los Angeles Temple on March 11, 1956, and the Oakland Temple on November 17, 1964.

Not long after the dedication of the Oakland Temple, plans were under way for three more temples, in Provo and Ogden, Utah, and in Washington, D.C.

In addition to his heavy responsibilities associated with the general jurisdiction of the Church, and throughout all his unselfish service whenever he was called to special duties, he never neglected individual members of the Church. Thousands were the recipients of his counsel and advice and were blessed by his administrations. His understanding of the human heart and his incomparable tenderness drew people close to him, and his deep interest in and concern for their welfare won for him the eternal love and respect of countless thousands.

In my day-to-day service I particularly observed and otherwise knew of many faith-promoting and inspiring incidents in the life of this great and noble man, brought about by sublime faith in God, by prayer, and through service. It has been my fervent hope throughout the years that others might share at least some of these "heart petals" associated with the life of President McKay.

The following faith-promoting experiences and other treasured materials, which I have gleaned from countless manuscripts of speeches and articles and from the personal scrapbooks of this revered Prophet, Seer, and Revelator, are but a few of those that have been recorded. They are given with the prayerful hope that consolation, encouragement, and increased faith may be gained by all who read what is herein compiled.

# Section I

## Memorable Testimonies

# What My Faith Means to Me

*Address delivered September 24, 1948.*

In the gospel plan, human life is divided into three periods or existences; viz., the preexistent state, the mortal state, and the antemortal state. The gospel of Jesus Christ is the true philosophy of these three states of being. It explains the *past*, is a guide to the *present*, unveils the *future*.

My faith gives me an assurance that God is indeed my Father, and that therefore I must have inherited his immortality. This explanation of my being is an anchor to my soul amid the unsettled, never-resting theories given in attempted explanations of the origin of man. So far as man's antemortal state is concerned, I rejoice in the revealed word that man was in the beginning with the Father. This is the truth glimpsed by the poet when he wrote:

> *The Soul that rises with us,*
> *Our life's Star,*
> *Hath had elsewhere its setting*
> *And cometh from afar;*
> *Not in entire forgetfulness,*
> *And not in utter nakedness,*
> *But trailing clouds of glory do we come*
> *From God, who is our home.*
>
> —William Wordsworth

My faith means an unfailing guide through this present existence, a final solution to life's perplexing problems. It gives to earth life a definite purpose. It teaches me that only through individual effort and divine guidance may true success and happiness be obtained. There is no blessing based upon another's achievement. Everyone must work out his own salvation. Life is a garden in which each person gathers the flowers and fruits from the seeds he plants. An abundant harvest is the result only of painstaking, intelligent effort.

The gospel includes all the conditions necessary for the

physical, intellectual, moral, and spiritual development of human life. Obedience to the gospel means merely compliance with the laws of health and happiness. It means keeping the body undefiled and the spirit in tune with the infinite.

The dearest possession a man has is his family. In the divine assurance that family ties may transcend the boundaries of death and may continue throughout endless ages of eternity, I find supreme consolation and inspiration. When the union of loved ones bears the seal of the Holy Priesthood, it is as eternal as love, as everlasting as spirit. Such a union is based on the doctrine of immortality and the eternal progress of man.

The church of Jesus Christ was established by the authority and through the personal administration of the Savior, who revealed to the Prophet Joseph Smith the true relationship of man to his Maker. Man is in spirit literally the offspring of Deity and as such has inherited the divine characteristics of the Father. Those traits are developed by obedience to the laws of life and being as revealed through the gospel of Jesus Christ.

# Predictions and Spiritual Manifestations

*Upon an invitation to reveal his innermost thoughts for the readers of the Deseret News Church Section, October 27, 1934, President McKay responded with the following.*

You ask me to let you look into my innermost feelings, and there reveal to you my intimate thoughts. Oliver Wendell Holmes says that every person's feelings have a front door and a side door by which they may be entered. Some people keep the front door always open; some keep it latched; some locked; some bolted with a chain that will let you peep in but not get in; and some nail it up so that nothing can pass its threshold. The side door opens at once into the sacred apartments. The key to this side door is carried for years hidden in a mother's bosom; sometimes fathers, brothers, and sisters,

President David O. McKay, the missionary. Taken while on his first
mission in Scotland, December 1897.

and friends have duplicates of it. The wedding ring conveys a right to one.

By complying with your request now I am handing you, for the time being, the key to this side door.

The first thing you will observe in that "sacred chamber" is a true sense of appreciation for the trust imposed in me by my close associates and by the Lord. Such confidence thus given is at once a sacred obligation. It implies loyalty and service to friends and to God. In turn I place my implicit trust in my Heavenly Father, who can substitute for weakness increased strength.

To give you a more intimate glimpse, however, I must tell you that recent events have given me a yearning to meet again my father and mother, just to tell them what their lives, their daily example, and willing sacrifices for their children have meant to me. I want to acknowledge to them my unpayable debt of eternal gratitude. I should like to see the expression on Mother's countenance as she would recall the following incident when I was a bouncing, boisterous baby. As related to me by her brother, my uncle, it is as follows:

"One day as I watched you toddling around on the floor, I teasingly made a deprecating remark about you. I remember your mother picked you up and said as she cuddled you to her cheek, 'You do not know, he may be an apostle some day.' "

Of course, it may have been, and undoubtedly was, just an expression of an ardent wish of a fond mother. All mothers hope for great things for their boys; but, oh, in my heart I have wished she might have lived to see her hopes fulfilled. However, I feel sure she knows, and it is quite possible she realizes now whether she expressed the wish of a hopeful mother or whether there was not with those hopes a flash of inspiration.

Another incident, however, seems to have carried deeper significance of inspiration. I was on my first mission, president, at the time, of the Scottish Conference in the year 1899. Presiding over the European Mission were Elders Platt D. Lyman, Henry W. Naisbitt, and James L. McMurrin. President McMurrin represented the European Mission presidency at a conference held in Glasgow,

Scotland. Following a series of meetings, we held a most remarkable priesthood meeting, one that will never be forgotten by any who was present.

I remember, as if it were but yesterday, the intensity of the inspiration of that occasion. Everybody felt the rich outpouring of the Spirit of the Lord. All present were truly of one heart and one mind. Never before had I experienced such an emotion. It was a manifestation for which as a doubting youth I had secretly prayed most earnestly on hillside and in meadow. It was an assurance to me that sincere prayer is answered "sometime, somewhere."

During the progress of the meeting, an elder on his own initiative arose and said, "Brethren, there are angels in this room." Strange as it may seem, the announcement was not startling; indeed, it seemed wholly proper, though it had not occurred to me there were divine beings present. I only knew that I was overflowing with gratitude for the presence of the Holy Spirit. I was profoundly impressed, however, when President James L. McMurrin arose and confirmed that statement by pointing to one brother sitting just in front of me and saying, "Yes, brethren, there are angels in this room, and one of them is the guardian angel of that young man sitting there," and he designated one who today is a patriarch of the Church.

Pointing to another elder, he said, "And one is the guardian angel of that young man there," and he singled out one whom I had known from childhood. Tears were rolling down the cheeks of both of these missionaries, not in sorrow or grief, but as an expression of the overflowing Spirit; indeed, we were all weeping.

Such was the setting in which James L. McMurrin gave what has since proved to be a prophecy. I had learned by intimate association with him that James McMurrin was pure gold, his faith in the gospel implicit; that no truer man, no more loyal man to what he thought was right ever lived. So when he turned to me and gave what I thought then was more of a caution than a promise, his words made an indelible impression upon me. Paraphrasing the words of the Savior to Peter, he said, "Let me say to you, Brother David, Satan hath desired you that he may sift you as wheat, but God is mindful of you." Then he added, "If you will keep the faith, you will yet sit in the leading councils of the Church." At that moment there flashed in my mind temptations that had beset my path, and I realized even better than President McMurrin, or any other man, how truly he had spoken when he said, "Satan hath desired thee." With the resolve then and there to keep the faith, there was born a desire to be of service to my fellowmen, and with it a realization, a glimpse at least, of what I owed to the elder who first carried the message of the restored gospel to my grandfather and grandmother who had accepted the message years before in the north of Scotland and in South Wales.

Following that meeting I had occasion to visit the scenes of my grandparents' childhood, and I more fully and completely comprehended what the gospel had done for them and for their descendants.

I know that these two incidents mean but little to others, but to me they connote so much that is intimately precious, and are so profoundly important as milestones in my life, that I cherish them as sacred possessions.

# The Prayer of a Youth

*As dictated by President McKay in 1938.*

One day in my youth I was hunting cattle. While climbing a steep hill, I stopped to let my horse rest, and there, once again, an intense desire came over me to receive a manifestation of the truth of the restored gospel. I dismounted, threw my reins over my horse's head, and there under a serviceberry bush I prayed that God would declare to me the truth of his revelation to Joseph Smith. I am sure that I prayed fervently and sincerely and with as much faith as a young boy could muster.

At the conclusion of the prayer, I arose from my knees, threw the reins over my faithful pony's head, and got into the saddle. As I started along the trail again, I remember saying to myself, "No spiritual manifestation has come to me. If I am true to myself, I must say I am just the same 'old boy' that I was before I prayed."

The Lord did not see fit to give me an answer on that occasion, but in 1899, after I had been appointed president of the Scottish Conference, the spiritual manifestation for which I had prayed as a boy in my teens came as a natural sequence to the performance of duty.

# A Testimony of Joseph Smith

*Address delivered at general priesthood meeting in the Salt Lake Tabernacle, October 6, 1951.*

I wish to bear you a testimony which I think I have never before given in public. Since childhood it has been very easy for me to believe in the reality of the visions of the Prophet Joseph Smith. This may seem very simple to you, but I give it as a heart petal.

When I was a very young child in the home of my youth, I was fearful at night. I traced it back to a vivid dream when two Indians (some Indians used to come near our home) came into the yard. I ran to the house for protection, and one of them shot an arrow and hit me in the back. Only a dream, but I felt that blow, and I was very much frightened, for in the dream they entered, one a tall one and the other a smaller one, and sneered and frightened Mother.

I never got over it. Added to that were the fears of Mother, for when Father was away with the herd or on some mission, Mother would never retire without looking under the bed; so burglars were real to me, or wicked men who would come in and attempt to injure Mother and the younger children.

Whatever the conditions, I was very fearful. One night I could not sleep. I was only a boy, and I fancied I heard noises around the house. Mother was away in another room. Thomas E. by my side was sleeping soundly. I could not sleep, and I became terribly fearful. I decided that I would do as my parents had taught me to do—pray. I thought I could not pray without getting out of bed and kneeling, and that was a terrible test. But I finally did bring myself to get out of bed and kneel and pray to God to protect Mother and the family. A voice as clear to me as mine is to you said, "Don't be afraid. Nothing will hurt you." Where it came from, what it was, I am not saying. You may judge. To me it was a direct answer, and there came an assurance that I should never be hurt in bed at night.

I say it has been easy for me to understand and believe the reality of the visions of the Prophet Joseph. It was easy for me in youth to accept his vision—the appearance of God the Father and his Son, Jesus Christ, to the boy praying. I could not think otherwise, for the vision is a reality. It was easy for me to believe that Moroni came to him there in his room. Heavenly beings were real from my babyhood on, and as years came those impressions were strengthened by reason and the inspiration of God directly to my soul.

I know that those visions were real and that Joseph Smith was a Prophet of God. This being true, it follows that Jesus Christ lives and is our Redeemer; that this is his church. We are merely his representatives, and when we acknowledge that this is his church, the reality of God the Father, the Father of our spirits, is very easy to accept.

These things being real, we cannot do anything else but try to our utmost to do what Jesus Christ, our Redeemer, asks us to do, for he has given us the gospel that bears his name, and in the words of Peter, "There is none other name under heaven given among men, whereby we must be saved." (Acts 4:12.)

# The Tenth Load

*Address delivered in the Salt Lake Temple Annex, September 25, 1941.*

What does it mean to obey the law of sacrifice? Nature's law demands that we do everything with self in view. The first law of mortal life, self-preservation, would claim the most luscious fruit, the most tender meat, the softest down on which to lie. Selfishness, the law of nature, would say, "I want the best; that is mine." But God said, "Take of the firstlings of your herds and of your flocks." (Deut. 12:6.)

The best shall be given to God; the next you may have. Thus should God become the center of our very being.

With this thought in view, I thank my earthly father for the lesson he gave to two boys in a hayfield at a time when tithes were paid in kind. We had driven out to the field to get the tenth load of hay, and then over to a part of the meadow where we had taken the ninth load, where there was "wire grass" and "slough grass." As we started to load the hay, Father called out, "No, boys, drive over to the higher ground." There was timothy and redtop there. But one of the boys called back (and it was I), "No, let us take the hay as it comes!"

"No, David, that is the *tenth* load, and the best is none too good for God."

That is the most effective sermon on tithing I have ever heard in my life, and it touches, I found later in life, this very principle of the law of sacrifice. You cannot develop character without obeying that law. Temptation is going to come to you in this life. You sacrifice your appetites; you sacrifice your passions for the glory of God; and you gain the blessing of an upright character and spirituality. That is a fundamental truth.

# Peace Through the Gospel of Christ

*In 1881, President McKay's father, Bishop David McKay, was called to serve as a missionary in Scotland, his native land. He was appointed president of the Glasgow District, and during this period of his life he had many interesting and faith-promoting experiences. One of these experiences relating to his testimony regarding the revelation that came to him of the divinity of the mission of the Prophet Joseph Smith is told by President McKay in the following address delivered at a fast meeting held September 28, 1919.*

It is indeed a privilege to meet and to commune not only with one another, but also with God our Eternal Father, being shut out from all the unrest and turmoil of the world. I think never before in my life have I seen such a contrast between the peace and contentment and assurance of the Latter-day Saints and the unrest, the strife, envy, and bitterness of the world. In the first section of the Doctrine and Covenants you will remember that the Lord refers to the tendency of the world to have different gods. They set up unto themselves their gods, which are after the fashion of the world. Has there ever been a time in the history of the world when men worshiped so many different gods after the fashion of the world—the god of greed, of selfishness, the god of sensuality? Why, it seems to me that every form of idol is now worshiped in preference to God, the Eternal Father, and men sacrifice everything for their earthly deities.

I testify to you, in all soberness, that God our Heavenly Father lives, that he communicates with his servants, that he has established in this dispensation of the world his great work, the only plan of salvation whereby mankind may be saved, the only means by which peace may be established in the world. Peace can come only when men will acknowledge God as their Creator, as their Father, and when they will obey the principles of the gospel of Jesus Christ and will have in their souls individual righteousness, a desire to reverence God, a desire to serve their fellowmen, a desire to bless the other man instead of bringing, at the expense of the other man, some benefit to themselves. The lines between truth and error are being more sharply drawn every day of our lives as never before. Any careful thinker may observe the present world turmoil and know for a surety the distinction between the peace of the gospel of Jesus Christ and the conflict and envy resulting from selfishness and strife. We must preach repentance, as the Prophet Joseph through inspiration declares in so many of his revelations, and declare also the restoration of the gospel of Jesus Christ.

I said to you that I know that the Lord communicates with his servants. I have not doubted this as a fact since I was a boy and heard the testimony of my father regarding the revelation that came to him of the divinity of the mission of the Prophet Joseph. I feel impressed to relate that circumstance and add his testimony to the one that I am now giving. He accepted a call to a mission in 1881. When he began preaching in his native land and bore testimony of the restoration of the gospel of Jesus Christ, he noticed that the people turned away from him. They were bitter in their hearts against anything Mormon, and the name of Joseph Smith seemed to arouse antagonism in their hearts. One day he concluded that the best way to reach these people would be to preach just the simple principles, the atonement of the Lord Jesus Christ, the first principles of the gospel, and not bear testimony of the restoration. In a month or so he became oppressed with a gloomy, downcast feeling, and he could not enter into the spirit of his work. He did not really know what was the matter, but his mind became obstructed; his spirit became depressed; he was oppressed and hampered; and that feeling of depression continued until it weighed him down with such heaviness that he went to the Lord and said, "Unless I can get this feeling removed, I shall have to go home. I can't continue having my work thus hampered."

The discouragement continued for some time after that, when, one morning before daylight, following a sleepless night, he decided to retire to a cave, near the ocean, where he knew he would be shut off from the world entirely, and there pour out his soul to God and ask why he was oppressed with this feeling, what he had done, and what he could do to throw it off and continue his work. He started out in the dark toward the cave. He became so eager to get to it that he started to run. As he was leaving the town, he was hailed by an officer who wanted to know what was the matter. He gave some noncommittal but satisfactory reply and was permitted to go on. Something just seemed to drive him; he had to get relief. He entered the cave or sheltered opening, and said, "Oh, Father, what can I do to have this feeling removed? I must have it lifted or I cannot continue in this work"; and he heard a voice, as distinct as the tone I am now uttering, say, "Testify that Joseph Smith is a prophet of God." Remembering then what he tacitly had decided six weeks or more before, and becoming overwhelmed with the thought, the whole thing came to him in a realization that he was there for a special mission, and he had not given that special mission the attention it deserved. Then he cried in his heart, "Lord, it is enough," and went out from the cave.

You who know him know the mission he performed. As a boy, I sat and heard that testimony from one whom I treasured and honored as you know I treasured no other man in the world, and that assurance was instilled in my youthful soul. The inspiration and the testimony of God has come since, and today I testify to you that God lives, that he is guiding this church, that he has inspired those at the head, and that he will continue to inspire them and lead them through the turmoil and unrest in the world caused by unrighteousness, wickedness, and lack of faith in God. Many people of the world do not believe in God; they do not believe in his principles; they have not applied his principles. They confess him with their lips, but their hearts have not been with him.

Let us thank our Heavenly Father for the testimony that the Lord Jesus Christ has placed in our souls. May we be true to that testimony, not only in words but also in acts, and show the world that we have the principles, obedience to which will establish peace on earth and good will among men. This is my prayer for all of us, in the name of Jesus Christ. Amen.

# A Room in Wales

*Excerpts from an address given August 24, 1952, at the dedication of the Brigham City Seventh Ward chapel, North Box Elder Stake.*

A short time ago—it does not seem possible that just a month ago—I stood in a little room in Wales, in which my mother was born one hundred and two years ago, the room so small that the six-foot bed covers the entire width, and in length barely two feet longer than it is wide, and the old rafters just two feet above my head, so about eight feet high. My thoughts on that occasion have been sacred to me. I shall share one or two with you.

I thought, as Sister McKay and I stood in that small bedroom, how different life would be now if two humble elders had not knocked at that door a hundred years ago! And how different life would be if my mother's father and mother had not accepted that message! I looked around the village and found descendants of

A winter scene of the McKay family home, Huntsville, Utah, January 1955.

Birthplace of Jennette Evans McKay, mother of President David O. McKay, in Plas-Helygen, Clwyd de fagyr, Cefn Coed Cymmer, near Merthyr Tydfil, South Wales. The picture was taken July 16, 1952. Standing left to right: President McKay, Emma Ray Riggs McKay; a distant cousin of President McKay, Blodwen Davies; Mildred Calderwood McKay, and David Lawrence McKay.

others who heard it at that time, descendants of some who ridiculed my grandfather and grandmother for having accepted the truth; who made light of their religion, scoffed at them, and ostracized them for having accepted Mormonism. I realized how unenlightened those neighbors were when they condemned my grandparents.

I recalled, as we stood there, what my grandmother said to me in Ogden, when she told me as a student in my teens about the experience she had when she left Cefn Coed. My mother's sister, Aunt Lizzie, the youngest of the children, had just been born when the eldest son was called away by death. My grandmother said, "I condemned the Lord in my heart for having taken away the one main help on the journey ahead of us, and I said, in my heart, 'Lord, if you had to take any of my children, why didn't you take this little helpless baby and leave us the oldest son to help us on the journey across the ocean and across the plains?'" When she told me that, she said, "I was wrong in my judgment. God knew best, and I should have trusted him. You see today how blessed I am living here with Lizzie, my youngest child, now the mother of three boys, and my comfort in my old age. God looked farther into the future than I could."

I remembered that statement, as I fancied I could hear the cry of my mother, born one hundred and two years before. Incidentally, acceptance of that gospel meant much to me—indeed I should not have been born, because that was in Wales and Father's folk were way up in the north of Scotland. It was only through the gospel that Father and Mother met. So I expressed gratitude, as I sensed it probably never so keenly before, as we stood in that little room.

On that occasion and following, I have thought of how many changes have taken place since August 1850. I believe that Edison was born three years earlier, in 1847. So all of his inventions have happened since then. There was no incandescent light; there was no phonograph. They had only the candle, probably the wick in grease, no bicycle, no automobiles, no airplanes—people had not even dreamed of them. They mowed their grass with the scythe, the grain with the "cradle"—no atom bomb, no steamships. When Mother, a young girl six years of age, crossed the ocean, it took thirty-nine days. Just recently we crossed the ocean, from Scotland to Newfoundland, in nine hours—fourteen hours from Glasgow to New York. Hours! Thirty-nine days then!

# "The Kingdom of God or Nothing"

*Written by President McKay at Ogden, Utah, January 2, 1915.*

Just above the pulpit in the meetinghouse where as a boy I attended Sunday services, there hung for many years a large photograph of the late President John Taylor, and under it, in what I thought were gold letters, this phrase:

The Kingdom of God or Nothing

The sentiment impressed me as a mere child years before I understood its real significance. I seemed to realize at that early date that there is no other church or organization that approaches the perfection or possesses the divinity that characterizes the church of Jesus Christ. As a child I felt this intuitively; in youth, I became thoroughly convinced of it; and today I treasure it as a firm conviction of my soul.

Another truth that I have cherished from childhood is that God is a personal Being and is, indeed, our Father whom we can approach in prayer and receive answers thereto. I cherish as one of the dearest experiences in life the knowledge that God hears the prayer of faith.

It is true that the answer may not come as direct and at the time or in the manner we anticipate; but it comes, and at a time and in a manner best for the interests of him who offers the supplication. On more than one occasion, I have received direct and immediate assurances that my petition has been granted. At one time particularly, the answer came as distinctly as though my father stood by my side and spoke the words. These experiences are part of my being and must remain so as long as memory and intelligence last. They have taught me that "heaven is never deaf but when man's heart is dumb."

Just as real and just as close to me seems the Savior of the world. He is God made manifest in the flesh; and I know that "there is none other name under heaven given among men, whereby we must be saved." (Acts 4:12.)

I have an abiding testimony that the Father and the Son appeared to the Prophet Joseph Smith and revealed through him the gospel of Jesus Christ, which is, indeed, "the power of God unto salvation." I know, too, that a knowledge of the truth of the gospel may be obtained only through obedience to the principles thereof. In other words, the best way to know the truth of any principle is to live it. Such is the way marked out by the Savior when he said, "If any man will do his will, he shall know of the doctrine, whether it be of God, or whether I speak of myself." (John 7:17.)

The divinity of The Church of Jesus Christ of Latter-day Saints is shown in its organization as well as in its teachings. Godhood, brotherhood, service—these three guiding principles in the Christ life permeate all our Church activity.

I love the work. I love the brethren who preside over it, for they are faithful and true men, performing their many duties under the inspiration of the Almighty.

In conclusion, I desire to testify to another thing: The Lord is not only guiding his church, but overruling the destiny of nations preparatory to the preaching of the gospel to every nation, kindred, tongue, and people. Dreadful as are the perilous conditions in war-torn countries today, we may rest assured that out of it all will come better opportunities for the honest men and women of the world to hear the "glad tidings of great joy" as heralded again in this the last and greatest of all dispensations. Out of the darkness now brooding over the nations, made more gloomy and terrible by the thunderings and tempests of war and bloodshed, will come the dawn of that long expected day when peace and good will will reign over all the earth.

Upon Latter-day Saints rests the responsibility of preaching the true gospel of peace to mankind. O may we be equal to this responsibility!

# Man Is But
# a Tenant of His
# Physical Body

*From the funeral address at the services for Mrs. William R. Calderwood, February 23, 1949.*

If we could look upon life as continuous and upon death as a mere incident in life, the pangs of parting would be less severe and the power of death would then be limited, as it is, only to the physical senses; it would be a liberator rather than a destroyer of the personal life of man.

Man is but a tenant of his physical body. This view was very impressively expressed by ex-President of the United States John Quincy Adams. He was met on the streets of Boston by a friend who inquired how he was feeling, and he answered, "Thank you! John Quincy Adams himself is well, sir, quite well. I thank you. But the house in which he lives at present is becoming dilapidated. It is tottering upon its foundations. Time and the seasons have nearly destroyed it. Its roof is pretty well worn out. Its walls are much shattered, and it trembles with every wind. The old tenement is becoming almost uninhabitable, and I think John Quincy Adams will have to move out of it soon; but he, himself, is quite well, sir, quite well."

The scriptures tell us that when this mortal shall put on immortality, then shall be brought to pass the saying, "Death is swallowed up in victory.

"O death, where is thy sting? O grave, where is thy victory?" (1 Cor. 15:54-55.)

# "Try the Spirits"

*From an address delivered by President McKay at the 102nd Semiannual General Conference of the Church, October 2, 1931.*

". . . believe not every spirit, but try the spirits whether they are of God. . . ." (1 John 4:1.)

It is wonderful to be anchored in the truth. When one is anchored to a testimony that God has spoken in this dispensation and that he has revealed his truth, there is little danger of one's becoming moved by any false theory, any half truth, or any false accusation that may be brought into his life. All such will affect one only as the waves affect immovable cliffs on the shore. But when one is not anchored, then he becomes easily moved, or at least unrestful and ill at ease. So it is necessary at all times to try the spirits, to make the test. Let the Church, the gospel of Jesus Christ, be the measuring rod. When things do not harmonize with the truths of the gospel we can pass them by, or at least hold them in abeyance until either truth or falsity be established.

My mind recently has been drawn to the importance of our people testing the spirit of slander, of calumny, and I would like to raise my voice in warning against such a spirit. It is easy to distinguish between the spirit of slander and the spirit of the gospel. I remember an instance in England during my late mission [President McKay presided over the European Mission, 1922-24] that may illustrate my meaning. Two elders had gone to great expense to procure a hall, announce their meeting, distribute literature, and so on. Their hopes were very high on Sunday morning as they approached that hired hall, for they saw a goodly number of persons accepting their invitation. One gentleman who was dressed in the garb of a Christian minister approached the hall and was greeted by the elder who was standing at the door. The latter extended his hand, but the minister refused, saying contemptuously, "I did not come here to shake hands with you."

"Very well," said the elder, "you are welcome," and he invited the minister into the hall.

When the elder reported this to me, he said, "I felt somewhat discouraged and gloomy."

I said, "You ought to be very thankful for the experience that came to you that morning. That gentleman misjudged you. You know he misjudged you. You know your sincerity. You know what you had in your heart. You know also that he was wrong in his accusation and in his feelings toward you and your people. Test that spirit and see if you have not more confidence in the work in which you are engaged than you ever had before."

And so, Latter-day Saints, test the spirit of the various accusations that are sometimes hurled against our leaders and against the Church. We have always had lies, calumny, and vituperation to fight, and the church of God will always have it. Our only problem is for us to be unmoved from our station.

The scriptures tell us: "Whoso privily slandereth his neighbour, him will I cut off. . . . He that worketh deceit shall not dwell within my house; he that telleth lies shall not tarry in my sight." (Ps. 101:5, 7.)

# The Sacred Door of Meditation

*From an address delivered by President McKay at the 116th Annual General Conference of the Church April 6, 1946.*

Before Jesus gave to the Twelve the beautiful Sermon on the Mount, he was in solitude, in communion. He did the same thing after that busy Sabbath day when he arose early in the morning, having been the guest of Peter. Peter undoubtedly found the guest chamber empty, and when he sought the Savior, he found him alone. It was on that morning that Peter said, "All men seek for thee." (Mark 1:37.)

Again, after Jesus had fed the five thousand, he told the Twelve to dismiss the multitude, but he went to the mountain for solitude. The historian says, ". . . and when the evening was come, he was there alone." (Matthew 14:23.) Meditation! Prayer!

I once read a book written by a very wise man, whose name I

cannot now recall, that contained a significant chapter on prayer. The author was not a member of the Church but evidently had a desire to keep in close communion with God, and he wanted to find the truth. Among other things he said, "In secret prayer go into the room, close the door, pull down the shades, and kneel in the center of the room. For a period of five minutes or so, say nothing. Just think of what God has done for you, of what are your greatest spiritual and temporal needs. When you sense that, and sense his presence, then pour out your soul to him in thanksgiving."

I believe the short period of administering the sacrament is one of the best opportunities we have for such meditation, and there should be nothing during that sacred period to distract our attention from the purpose of that ordinance.

One of the most impressive services I have ever attended was in a group of over eight hundred people to whom the sacrament was administered, and during that administration not a sound could be heard excepting the ticking of the clock—eight hundred souls, each of whom had the opportunity of communion with the Lord. There was no distraction, no orchestra, no singing, no speaking. Each one had an opportunity to search himself introspectively and to consider his worthiness or unworthiness to partake of the sacrament. His was the privilege of getting closer to his Father in heaven. That is ideal!

We recommend that we surround this sacred ordinance with more reverence, with perfect order, that each one who comes to the house of God may meditate upon God's goodness and silently and prayerfully express appreciation for his goodness. Let the sacrament hour be one experience of the day in which the worshiper tries at least to realize within himself that it is possible for him to commune with God.

Great events have happened in this church because of such communion, because of the responsiveness of the soul to the inspiration of the Almighty. I know it is real. President Wilford Woodruff had that gift to a great extent. He could respond; he knew the "still small voice" to which some are still strangers. You will find that when these most inspirational moments come to you, you are alone with yourself and your God. They come to you probably when you are facing a great trial, when the wall is across your pathway and it seems that you are facing an insurmountable obstacle, or when your heart is heavy because of some tragedy in your life. I repeat, the greatest comfort that can come to us in this life is to sense the realization of communion with God.

These secret prayers, these conscientious moments in meditation, these yearnings of the soul to reach out to feel the presence of God—such are the privileges of those who hold the Melchizedek Priesthood and of all other members who need help and guidance from the Lord.

God help us so to live that we may sense the reality, as I bear you my testimony that it is real, that we *can* commune with our Father in heaven. If we so live to be worthy of the companionship of the Holy Spirit, he will guide us into all truth; he will show us things to come; he will bring all things to our remembrance; he will testify of the divinity of the Lord Jesus Christ, as I do, and of the restoration of the gospel.

# How to Obtain Divine Guidance

*From an address given by President McKay at the Founder's Day ceremonies at Brigham Young University, Provo, Utah, October 16, 1936.*

The first condition in receiving divine guidance is the knowledge that we are more than a mere accumulation of physical particles. Every intelligent person knows this, particularly those who are born under the covenant and who are thus entitled to that blessing and guidance of the Holy Spirit.

The second condition is a realization of our own relationship to our Father in heaven—a realization that he loves us, that we are divine beings, that we are equal to others as far as God and our parents have given us intelligence, and that our soul has unlimited possibilities, particularly if we can be guided by inspiration, if we can become a part of that infinite whole, if we can have the guiding light of the Holy Spirit.

The third condition is a spontaneous desire, a longing of the soul for something. I can best explain this by an illustration. Following World War I, a young man said, "I had always looked upon prayer as an affront to the Most High, but one day when earth and sky seemed to be mingling with the grueling that we got from enemy guns, and I saw my men falling all around me, I cried out in my heart, 'O God, save my life for my men's sake.' The little bit of ribbon that I received for my service in battle is a symbol of that prayer. I think it should be deposited in some church. It seems sacred, for whenever I look at it, it reminds me of my prayer."

After that experience, prayer was not an affront in the mind of that boy. He prayed not for himself, but that he might help somebody else.

# Emulating the Examples of Great Men

*From an address by President McKay at the 121st Annual General Conference, April 8, 1951. He was sustained the next day at a solemn assembly in the Salt Lake Tabernacle as the ninth President of the Church.*

"For I know that my redeemer liveth, and that he shall stand at the latter day upon the earth:

"And though after my skin worms destroy this body, yet in my flesh shall I see God:

"Whom I shall see for myself, and mine eyes shall behold, and not another; though my reins be consumed within me." (Job 19:25-27.)

Thus was spoken the heartfelt assurance of Job, expressed in humiliation when everything else was taken from him and even his body utterly wasted in affliction.

If a few more million men in the world could feel that testimony—the testimony of the reality of our Redeemer—selfishness would be less manifest, war among nations would be eradicated, and peace would reign among mankind. Do you believe that, my fellow workers?

"What think ye of Christ?" was the question Jesus put to a group of Pharisees when they, with scribes and Sadducees, sought to entrap and confound the Great Teacher by asking him entangling questions. He silenced the Sadducees in their attempt to ensnare him with regard to paying tribute to Caesar. He satisfied the scribes regarding the first and great commandment. Now he put to silence the Pharisees regarding their anticipated Christ.

To this congregation, to the Church, and to the world, I repeat this question as being the most vital, the most far-reaching query in this unsettled, distracted world.

Great minds in all ages who have contributed to the betterment of mankind have been inspired by noble ideals.

History is replete with men who, as Wordsworth expresses it, "by the vision splendid, were on their way attended." There is John Milton, for example, inspired with a desire as a boy of twelve to write a poem that would live for centuries. As a result, the world has *Paradise Lost*; and later in life, though blind, the poet as he approached the closing moments of his life exclaimed: "Still guides the heavenly vision!" Sir Walter Scott wrote almost day and night to pay off a debt for which he was not really responsible.

George Washington, guided by the desire to build a noble character and to be of service to his country, cried: "I hope I may always have firmness and virtue enough to maintain what I consider to be the most enviable of all titles—the character of an honest man." Abraham Lincoln expressed himself thus: ". . . with malice toward none, with charity for all, with firmness in the right as God gives us to see the right, let us strive on to finish the work we are in, to bind up the nation's wounds, to care for him who shall have borne the battle, and for his widow and his orphan to do all which may achieve and cherish a just and lasting peace among ourselves and with all nations."

These and others who live to their best are the men "who realize in daily life their luminous hours and transmute their ideals into conduct and character. These are," continues the writer, "the soul architects, who build their thoughts and deeds into a plan; who travel forward, not aimlessly, but toward a destination; who shall not any-whither but toward a port, who steer not by the clouds, but by fixed stars. High in the scale of manhood these who ceaselessly aspire towards life's Great Exemplar."

But the highest of all ideals are the teachings and particularly the life of Jesus of Nazareth, and that man is most truly great who is most Christlike.

What you sincerely in your heart think of Christ will determine what you are, will largely determine what your acts will be. No person can study this divine personality, can accept his teachings without becoming conscious of an uplifting and refining influence within himself. In fact, every individual may experience the operation of the most potent force that can affect humanity.

# Honoring Our Pioneer Forefathers

*In 1938 President McKay was appointed by Governor Henry H. Blood of Utah to be chairman of the Centennial Commission to direct planning for the centennial celebration honoring the arrival of the pioneers in the Salt Lake Valley in 1847. At a centennial program in the Salt Lake Tabernacle April 16, 1947, President McKay gave the following tribute.*

The best way to honor the pioneers is to emulate and make practical in our lives the ideals and virtues that strengthened and animated their lives. These eternal ideals and principles that they fostered and upheld, even under the most adverse conditions, are as applicable today as they were when emphasized by the pioneer leaders.

I should like to take time today to refer to only a few. As I name them, will you please mentally point out their applicability to present world conditions.

Foremost was their outstanding faith in the Lord Jesus Christ and in his restored gospel. The very first instruction given when they began their journey across the plains was that they should pray morning and night and keep the Sabbath day holy. When they arrived in the valley, to quote the words of President Brigham Young, they prayed "over the land and dedicated it and the water, air, and everything pertaining to them unto the Lord, and the smiles of heaven rested upon the land and it became productive."

Among the outstanding virtues of the pioneers were industry and thrift. They condemned idleness and wastefulness as not being in accordance with the rules of heaven. Said President Young: "My experience has taught me, and it has become a principle with me, that it is never any benefit to give, out and out, to man or woman, money, food, clothing, or anything else, if they are able-bodied, and can work and earn what they need, when there is anything on earth, for them to do. This is my principle, and I try to act upon it. To pursue a contrary course would ruin any community in the world and make them idlers. . . .To give to the idler is as wicked as anything else." (*Discourses of Brigham Young* [Deseret Book, 1946], pp. 274-75.)

To the pioneers, marriage was ordained of God. It was not something that should be entered into lightly, terminated at pleasure, or ended at the first difficulty that might arise. They taught that the marriage bond should be as eternal as love, the most divine attribute of the human soul. Most surely, then, that bond should continue as long as love is an attribute of the spirit. Said President Young:

"Let every man in the land over eighteen years of age take a wife, and then go to work with your hands and cultivate the earth, or labor at some mechanical business, or some honest trade to provide an honest living for yourselves and those who depend upon you for their subsistence; observing temperance and loving truth and virtue; then would the woman be cared for, be nourished, honored, and blest, becoming honorable mothers of a race of men and women farther advanced in physical and mental perfection than their fathers. This would create a revolution in our country, and would produce results that would be of incalculable good." (*Discourses*, pp. 194-95.)

What was their idea regarding chastity and virtue? As fundamental to domestic happiness and social uplift, they cherished these ideals. Said President Young on one occasion:

"Any man who humbles a daughter of Eve to rob her of her virtue and cast her off dishonored and defiled, is her destroyer, and is responsible to God for the deed. If the refined Christian society of the nineteenth century will tolerate such a crime, God will not; but he will call the perpetrator to account. He will be damned; in hell he will lift up his eyes, being in torment, until he has paid the uttermost farthing, and made full atonement for his sins.

"The defiler of the innocent is the one who should be branded with infamy and cast out from respectable society, and shunned as a pest, or, as a contagious disease, is shunned. The doors of respectable families should be closed against him, and he should be frowned upon by all high-minded and virtuous persons. Wealth, influence and position should not screen him from their righteous indignation. His sin is one of the blackest in the calendar of crime, and he should be cast down from the high pinnacle of respectability and consideration to find his place among the worst of felons." (*Discourses*, p. 194.)

Those pioneers condemned the artificial means of limiting the number of children in the family, a growing evil, not only throughout the United States but also here in our own settlements. Said the great leader: "To check the increase of our race has its advocates among the influential and powerful circles of society in our nation and in other nations. . . . The unnatural style of living, the extensive use of narcotics, the attempts to destroy and dry up the fountains of life, are fast destroying the American element of the nation. . . ." (*Discourses*, p. 197.)

Regarding self-control, the pioneers voiced the teachings of the Church on this principle: "Let each person be determined, in the name of the Lord Jesus Christ, to overcome every besetment—to be the master of himself, that the spirit God has put in your tabernacles shall rule; then you can converse, live, labor, go here or there, do this or that, and converse and deal with your brethren as you ought.

"You cannot inherit eternal life, unless your appetites are brought in subjection to the spirit that lives within you, the spirit which our Father in Heaven gave. I mean the Father of your spirits, of those spirits which he has put into these tabernacles. The tabernacle must be brought into subjection to the spirit perfectly, or your bodies cannot be raised to inherit eternal life; if they do come forth, they must'dwell in a lower kingdom. Seek diligently, until you bring all into subjection to the law of Christ.

"We often hear people excuse themselves for their uncouth manners and offensive language, by remarking, 'I am no hypocrite,' thus taking to themselves credit for that which is really no credit to them. When evil arises within me, let me throw a cloak over it, subdue it, instead of acting it out upon the false presumption that I am honest and no hypocrite. Let not thy tongue give utterance to the evil that is in thine heart, but command thy tongue to be silent until good shall prevail over the evil, until thy wrath has passed away and the good Spirit shall move thy tongue to blessings and words of kindness. . . . When my feelings are aroused to anger by the ill-doings of others, I hold them as I would hold a wild horse, and I gain the victory. Some think and say that it makes them feel better when they are mad, as they call it, to give vent to their madness in abusive and unbecoming language. This, however, is a mistake. Instead of its making you feel better, it is making bad worse. When you think and say it makes you better you give credit to a falsehood. When the wrath and bitterness of the human heart are moulded into words and hurled with violence at one another, without any check or hindrance, the fire has no sooner expended itself than it is again re-kindled through some trifling course, until the course of nature is set on fire. . . ." (*Discourses,* pp. 265-66.)

On slander the pioneers held this:

"Some are in the habit of talking about their neighbors, of vending stories they know nothing about, only that Aunt Sally said that Cousin Fanny told Aunt Betsy that old Aunt Ruth said something or other, or somebody had had a dream; and by the time the story or dream reaches you, it has assumed the semblance of a fact, and you are very foolishly spending your time in talking about things that amount to nothing, or that you have no concern with. A report is started that such a one has done wrong, and, by the time it has gone its rounds, has become anointed with the salve of the backbiter and tale-bearer—become endowed with their spirit. . . .

When you know what right is, and are capable of correcting a person that is wrong, then it is time enough for you to judge." (*Discourses*, p. 268.)

In this connection they condemned profanity: "If any are in the habit of taking the name of God in vain, cease doing so today, tomorrow and throughout the coming week, and so continue, and you will soon gain strength to overcome the habit entirely; you will gain power over your words." (*Discourses*, p. 268.)

So taught the father of our country, George Washington, who said to his soldiers on one occasion: "The general is sorry to be informed that the foolish and wicked practice of profane cursing and swearing, a vice heretofore little known in an American army, is growing in fashion. He hopes the officers will, by example as well as influence, endeavor to check it and that both they and the men will reflect that we can have little hope of the blessings of heaven on our arms if we insult it by our impiety and folly. Added to this, profanity is a vice so mean and low, without any temptation, that every man of sense and character detests and despises it."

The pioneers helped each other in adversity, shared with the hungry the last loaf of bread, gave their time and means for the upbuilding of the community, and on not a few occasions offered their lives for the truth. That is service.

Thus they exemplified in their teachings the two great commandments—love the Lord thy God with all thy might, mind, and strength, and thy neighbor as thyself. Truly they followed the example of the Prophet Joseph, who was ever an inspiration to the great leader of the Mormon pioneers. He said, "If my life is of no value to my friends, it is of no value to me."

Truly, in this centennial celebration, we can re-echo the words of the great composer, Evan Stephens:

*Zion's children sing for joy,*
*Praise the great and guiding hand*
*That led you to the chosen land,*
*Oh, dauntless pioneers!*

*Sing His praise who made you free*
*In the land of liberty,*
*Thank the Lord, who raised a band,*
*Of noble pioneers.*

*Zion's children shout for joy,*
*Make the hills and valleys ring,*
*Great the theme the song ye sing,*
*Immortal pioneers.*

God give us the power to perpetuate their faith and ideals, and thus help make their lives and deeds an everlasting blessing.

# "Greater Love Hath No Man"

*Article concerning a talk given by President McKay at the dedicatory services of the Berlin-Charlottenburg chapel in the West German Mission, adapted from an article in the* Millennial Star, *October 1958.*

Monday, September 8, was President McKay's birthday. In the afternoon session, each speaker had expressed his love for and testimony of him. President McKay hadn't intended to speak on that occasion, but he then felt compelled to do so. He acknowledged the birthday remembrance, and, more importantly, the love they represented; he said he was especially thankful that day for his mother. He would have spoken of her had the depth of his emotion not been too great to allow it.

The prophet wept quietly. No description can express his stature or his sweetness in those moments. Those who witnessed wept with him. And then he spoke—with mightiness, as a prophet speaks—of brotherhood and of the Savior.

He talked about the time of Joseph Smith's last imprisonment in Carthage Jail, and how much love the men present had for one another. They had kept their lives and associations pure, and now in the oppressive hours before the Prophet's tragedy, their bonds of brotherhood were stronger than the threat of death. John Taylor sang "A Poor Wayfaring Man of Grief," and the Prophet Joseph requested that he sing it again.

Here President McKay quoted the hymn in its entirety, speaking deliberately, in his singular way, filling each word to the utmost measure of its meaning. On his lips the language seemed liberated of its limitations: more even by his compelling combination of pureness and maturity than by his eloquence, and yet more by the power of his prophethood and the Spirit of God, as his words penetrated those who listened.

He continued, telling about Dr. Willard Richards and how Joseph had asked him, following their last meal in the jail, "If we go into the cell, will you go in with us?" The doctor answered, "Brother Joseph, you did not ask me to cross the river with you. You did not ask me to come to Carthage. You did not ask me to come to jail with you. Do you think I would forsake you now? But I will tell you what I will do; if you are condemned to be hung for treason, I will be hung in your stead, and you shall go free." Joseph said, "You cannot." The doctor replied, "I will."

President McKay told of Sydney Carton, who in Dickens' *A Tale of Two Cities* died as Willard Richards would have died, saying, "It's a far, far better thing I do now than I have ever done." We who were present had heard or read of the understanding of the world's learned and celebrated men—but, greater than they, here was a man before us who actually understood the meaning of the word *brotherhood* and of the word *love*. And here were a group of men sitting behind him, some of the General Authorities of the Church, who understood also, for they too wept. Their lives and associations they had kept pure, and the love they emanated was like the love about which he spoke.

He went on to talk of Jesus: how matchless was his love to have laid down his life for us. In President McKay's eyes were tears, most glorious to see; and he spoke, as it were, with the wholeness of his soul: "We wouldn't have anything, if it were not for Jesus. We wouldn't be here today, or have this gospel in our lives, or enjoy the association of our loved ones. . . ."

And we too wept to glimpse in that moment some of what David O. McKay knows in his heart about the Savior of mankind and to understand more perfectly the scripture, "As the Father hath loved me, so I have loved you: continue ye in my love. If ye keep my commandment, ye shall abide in my love; even as I have kept my Father's commandments, and abide in his love. These things have I spoken unto you, that my joy might remain in you, and that your joy might be full. This is my commandment, That ye love one another, as I have loved you. Greater love hath no man than this, that a man lay down his life for his friends." (John 15:9-13.)

We knew that no man could speak as David O. McKay had spoken, but that he too had given his life to serve his friends. His hearers at the six dedicatory sessions—British, French, Swiss, German, Norwegian, Dutch, Swedish, Danish, American, Finnish—listened, and love him deeply. If this is possible, merely on beholding and hearing him, how great shall be our love for our Father in heaven, if we are worthy to stand in his presence. And if we, in our weakness and shortcomings, can feel his pure love flow from him to us, how sublime and glorious shall be the love of God?

We have sensed more fully the reality of the personality of God, our Father, and of his Son, Jesus Christ, by beholding in President McKay a lofty stage in the maturity of the divine potential in men. We were able to say in our hearts, This man hath God ordained his spokesman: and we have known an unbridled and indescribable joy in his presence, have felt pure peacefulness and hope at his counsel—how much to be desired then is the peace and joy we may one day feel, if we live worthily, in the presence of him who sent this prophet?

# God Bless the
# Missionary Cause

*From an address delivered at the 139th Annual General Conference of the Church on Saturday, October 4, 1969, the last general priesthood session that President McKay addressed.*

In order to bring peace to the hearts of men in the world, take this message, my brethren. The people you teach must have these great truths in mind:

*First, faith in the Lord Jesus Christ, and acceptance of him as the Only Begotten Son of the Father, who came and redeemed all men from death and who established the principles of the gospel, by obedience to which men may gain salvation in his kingdom.* As Peter said before the judges in the Sanhedrin, ". . . there is none other name under heaven given among men, whereby we must be saved." (Acts 4:12.) Young men, take that message and instill faith in the hearts of the people of the world in God our Father and in his Son, Jesus Christ—faith that Christ's church has been established in this age, through the Prophet Joseph Smith, as he established it in the former days when Peter, James, and John lived as leaders.

*Second, kindness toward all men.* You cannot have enmity in your hearts toward any one person. Some may try to deprive you of your privileges, but you must keep kindness in your heart and prove to the world that you have the spirit of the lowly Nazarene who preached to the poor on the Sea of Galilee. With faith, with kindness, let your heart be filled with the desire to serve all mankind. The spirit of the gospel comes from service in the good of others. Listen to that paradoxical saying of the Son of Man: "For whosoever will save his life shall lose it; but whosoever shall lose his life for my sake and the gospel's, the same shall save it." (Mark 8:35.)

My dear young brethren of the Aaronic Priesthood, prepare for that day when you will go out into the world to preach the gospel of Jesus Christ; and, as you prepare, you will so radiate that you will truly be missionaries here at home, here and now.

The responsibility of the Church is to preach the gospel of

Jesus Christ as restored to the Prophet Joseph Smith, but not only to preach it and proclaim it by word and by distribution of literature, but more than anything else, to live the gospel in our homes and in our business dealings, have faith and testimony in our hearts, and radiate it wherever we go.

Brethren, there is nothing that can stop the progress of truth except our weaknesses or failure to do our duty.

In conclusion, let me urge more diligence in living and radiating the principles of the gospel. The older I grow, the more thrilled and more grateful I am for the church of Jesus Christ and the more impressed I am with the importance of declaring this truth to the world.

God bless the missionary cause, not merely to increase our membership, which will follow inevitably, but also to declare the restoration of the gospel of Jesus Christ and the divinity of the life, death, and resurrection of our Lord and Savior. Upon you, my fellow workers, and the millions of members of the Church, rests the responsibility of declaring to the world the divinity and divine Sonship of Jesus Christ.

Now, there are many who believe it is true; there are millions of honest souls who believe it—but they need men and women who will declare it, and declare that they have a testimony of that truth.

I bear you that testimony tonight. I know our Lord and Savior is at the head of this church and that he is guiding it. I know it as I know I live. I know that he with his Father restored this gospel as it was given in the meridian of time in its simplicity, in its beauty, in its divinity. I know that these brethren, constituting the General Authorities, are true servants of the Lord. I know that there are thousands—hundreds of thousands—of men and women in the Church who have that testimony. I pray that we may use the means that have been put into our hands to harvest the rich group of souls waiting to hear this message. Paul said he heard a voice calling him over into Macedonia, and he went into Europe and found honest souls waiting. We hear the voice calling, not only in Europe and Macedonia, but here at home and in the uttermost ends of the earth, "Come and give us the gospel."

God help us to heed that call and to answer it, that we may harvest the crop of honest souls to the glory of our Father, who said, "For behold, this is my work and my glory—to bring to pass the immortality and eternal life of man." (Moses 1:39.)

# I Leave My Blessing with You

*Address delivered at the closing session of the 137th Semiannual General Conference of the Church, held in the Salt Lake Tabernacle, October 1, 1967.*

I give you my testimony that God lives; that he is close to us; that his Spirit is real; that his voice is real; that Jesus Christ, his Son, stands at the head of this great work; and no matter how much of the atheistic philosophy takes hold of the blinded boys and girls and men and women who hear Satan's voice, the truth stands as declared by the Father and the Son to the boy prophet. You and I, and all true members of The Church of Jesus Christ of Latter-day Saints, have the responsibility to declare that truth to the world; and the world is full of honest men and women waiting to hear that truth. Let us not condemn them. Condemn the evil men who would blind them with their sophistry and with false reasoning. Some of our young people are so blinded, but it is our duty as officers of the Church to lead them from the things of the world.

It is the responsibility of every member of the Church to preach the restored gospel to every nation, kindred, tongue, and people, that the evils of the world may be met by the counteracting forces of truth.

When do temptations come? They come to us in our social gatherings; they come to us at our weddings; they come to us in our politics; they come to us in our business relations; they come to us on the farm and in the mercantile establishment, and in our dealings in the affairs of life. It is when they manifest themselves to the consciousness of each individual that the defense of truth ought to exert itself. There may never come a greater opportunity to defend this church.

When that still small voice calls to the performance of duty, insignificant though it seems, and its performance unknown to anyone save the individual and God, he who responds gains corresponding strength. Temptation often comes in the same quiet way. Perhaps the yielding to it may not be known by anyone save the individual and his God, but if he does yield to it, he becomes to that extent weakened and spotted with the evil of the world.

It is the unseen influence at work in society that is undermining the manhood and womanhood of today. It is these unseen influences that come from the world that overcome us when we are least prepared to defend ourselves. When we do not withstand the encroachments of these evil influences, we weaken the possibility of defending the church of Jesus Christ. This is an individual work, and what the individuals are, the aggregate is.

God bless you, my dear fellow workers. Bless you in your homes, and make your faith shown by your works in your home. Husbands, be true to your wives, not only in act, but in thought. Wives, be true to your husbands. Children, be true to your parents; do not arrogate to yourselves that they are old-fashioned in their beliefs and that you know more than they do. Girls, follow that sweet mother and her teachings. Boys, be true to your fathers, who want happiness and success for you which come only through living the principles of the gospel. Strangers, seeing such homes, will say, "Well, if that is the result of Mormonism, I think it is good." You will show by your faith and acts in everyday life what you really are.

Just to be associated with you, with men striving toward such an aim, is a joy; and to assist you in this quest, an inspiration. Unselfishly you are trying to serve your fellowmen in love. You are true followers of the Master, for to those who have the Christian faith, the most sublime of his teachings, and to him who penetrates its deepest sense, the most human concern of all is this: to save mankind, the Lord God came to dwell among us in the form of man and was willing to make himself known by this simple, though glorious, principle—*love*.

The animal world is filled with selfishness, each thing seeking its own life, its own perpetuation. But Christ lived for love: "Thou shalt love the Lord thy God with all thy heart, and with all thy soul, and with all thy mind. . . . And . . . Thou shalt love thy neighbor as thyself." (Matthew 22:37, 39.)

God bless the elders and the sisters who, if not with perfect love, at least with a desire to bring joy and peace to others, are engaged in the noblest calling of life. Worthy servants of Christ you are! Our teachers are followers of the true Redeemer, our Lord. There is nothing greater than this noble work, none more righteous. Yours is the joy promised by the Savior, who said:

"And if it so be that you should labor all your days in crying repentance unto this people, and bring, save it be one soul unto me, how great shall be your joy with him in the kingdom of my Father!

"And now, if your joy will be great with one soul that you have brought unto me into the kingdom of my Father, how great will be your joy if you should bring many souls unto me!" (D&C 18:15-16.)

God bless you men of the priesthood. May you hold it in dignity and righteousness which comes from within, not from without. To hold the priesthood of God by divine authority is one of the greatest gifts that can come to a man. He is greatly blessed who feels the responsibility of representing Deity. He should feel it to such an extent that he is conscious of his actions and words under all conditions.

God bless our friends who are contributing to the advancement of this great church. We are grateful for their friendship and goodwill.

God bless us that we may have a firmer resolve than we have ever had before to live the gospel of Jesus Christ, to be kind to our families and to our neighbors, to be honest in all our dealings so that men seeing our good works may be led to glorify our Father in heaven.

I leave my blessings with you, with the sick and afflicted, with our men in the service, and with our missionaries scattered around the world. I pray that God's protecting care will be with them wherever they are.

God bless you officers and leaders, stake presidencies and bishoprics of the Church. May the love of the Redeemer be in each heart, and that means that the love will be expressed in serving one another.

God bless these brethren of the General Authorities for their devotion and untiring efforts in furthering his work on earth. May they be blessed with increased health and strength to carry on their great responsibilities throughout the world.

I know that God lives; that his Son, Jesus Christ, is the Savior of the world; and that divine beings restored to the Prophet Joseph Smith the gospel of Jesus Christ as he established it in the meridian of time.

I bear this testimony as we part this afternoon, and pray the blessings of the Lord to be upon each of you; that the influence of the priesthood quorums, of auxiliaries, and of the missionaries may be more effective from this time forward than ever before in leading the honest in heart of the whole world to turn their hearts to the worship of God and give them power to control the animal nature and live in the Spirit, in the name of Jesus Christ. Amen.

# Section II

## Experiences During World Travels

# The Protection of the President in His Travels

By Clare Middlemiss

From that day in December 1920, when Presidents Heber J. Grant, Anthon H. Lund, Charles W. Penrose, and several of the apostles laid their hands upon President McKay's head and blessed him and set him apart as "a missionary to travel around the world" and promised him that he should be "warned of dangers seen and unseen, and be given wisdom and inspiration from God to avoid all the snares and the pitfalls that may be laid for his feet," that he should also "go forth in peace, in pleasure and happiness and to return in safety to his loved ones and to the body of the Church," he experienced the protecting care of our Heavenly Father in all his global ministry. In referring to the above blessing, he said in a report to the First Presidency in December 1921, "As promised by President Grant, we have traveled in peace, in pleasure and happiness, and have returned in safety to our loved ones and to the body of the Church. His blessing that I should have power over disease, not only in my own person but also through the power of the Almighty upon the sick and afflicted in the various missions, has been wonderfully, I might say miraculously, realized. We have truly been warned of dangers and, through inspiration, have avoided snares that would have proved at least discomforting, if not injurious."

Upon his return from his epoch-making tour of the European missions from May 29 to July 26, 1952, President McKay said, "We are grateful, first, for the protecting care, guiding hand, and divine inspiration of our Heavenly Father."

In 1955 when President McKay returned from his visit to the missions of the South Pacific, he reported that he recognized the overruling Providence in regard to their health; that it was significant that Sister McKay and he had made that trip, taking boats, seaplanes, airplanes, being entertained at various places, going without the necessary sleep, and through it all had returned home without any illness or distress. He said that the prayers of the brethren and the members of the Church were literally answered in their behalf. He further said that not once did any of their planned meetings or entertainments have to be cancelled because of storm, though when they were in Suva it rained four inches in one night, and it also rained in other places.

On many other occasions the elements were tempered in order that assignments might be carried out and destinations reached.

In Bern, Switzerland, in 1953, it had been raining six weeks prior to the date of the dedication of the temple site. After prayer and fasting by the missionaries and Saints, on the day of the dedication, Wednesday, August 5, 1953, the sun came out, the clouds disappeared, and there was a beautiful day for the open-air meeting. However, that night it started to rain again, and it rained all the following day. "Surely," said President McKay, "the prayers for good weather during the dedicatory services were answered." In London there was a similar experience. When it came time to dedicate the London Temple site, although it had rained steadily previous to the date of the dedication, bright, clear weather prevailed throughout the dedicatory services held on August 10, 1953.

Franklin J. Murdock, in his day-by-day journal of President and Sister McKay's 45,000-mile journey by air to Australia, New Zealand, and the islands of the South Pacific, said, "How fortunate we have been all along the way! It just seems that a protecting hand has gone ahead and directed the hurricanes in another direction as we needed to land, and even though we are in the rainy season, the weather for all occasions has been clear and warm, and not one meeting has had to be changed or broken up because of inclement weather. Good weather has been where we needed it to carry out the assignments, and the members have marveled at the sudden changes in the weather as each meeting or assignment has started. Surely the Lord is with us and has blessed us with good health, good spirits, and good protection!

"On January 15, 1955, the day of the dedication of the Church edifice at Sauniatu, Samoa, and the open-air services held at the David O. McKay Monument, although it had been raining previously, we encountered beautiful weather. As we bade farewell to the happy faces at Sauniatu and took a last glance at the monument, the rains started; but the meetings were completed, and we were safely in the automobile ready to drive back to Apia."

Elder Howard B. Stone, president of the Samoan Mission, reported the following concerning President and Sister McKay's visit to Samoa:

"The night before we landed at Aitutaki in the Cook Island group, January 18, 1955, Elders Bushoff and Johnson, with sixty-six Saints and eighty-five nonmembers, had traveled a distance of ten miles in three whaleboats and had slept under the stars and palm trees so that they could meet with President McKay and his party the next day for one short hour while the seaplane was refueling prior to its departure for Tahiti. We held a meeting in the grove of palm trees on that little island, after which all of the natives, who, incidentally, were very shy, quietly walked by in single file to shake hands with the Prophet of God and other members of the party. We were threatened with rain for the second time in a week, but in each instance, after a prayer in our hearts, a rainbow appeared in the horizon, and the rainstorm passed over us."

On January 31, 1955, just before President McKay and his traveling companions left Sydney, Australia, by plane for Brisbane, Australia, one of the missionaries, a member of the party, offered a prayer at the airport asking for God's protection on their journey. How well that prayer was answered is indicated in the following report by Elder Murdock:

"The trip from Sydney to Brisbane was made in a DC-4. The journey was smooth and without incident until we had been going for about an hour and a half. We were traveling at about 250 miles an hour. President Waters, a counselor in the mission presidency, had gone up into the cockpit with the pilot, who had agreed to circle over Brisbane in order that we could get a look at the city lighted up at night.

"Suddenly the pilot noticed a heavy rain and lightning storm in our pathway and seemed greatly concerned as to what the consequences might be. As the plane neared the storm area, the lights in the plane suddenly went out and then on, and the storm had disap-

President and Sister McKay upon their arrival at Mascot Aerodrome, Sydney, Australia, February 5, 1955.

peared. The pilot could not understand what had happened nor where the storm had gone, but it had vanished, and the plane went on its course without further incident."

Thus this worldwide missionary, who constantly sought the Lord with all his soul and who was deeply conscious of his dependence upon him for guidance and assistance, had the protecting care of our Heavenly Father throughout all his travels.

# A Touching Farewell

*On Saturday, December 4, 1920, Elder David O. McKay of the Council of the Twelve, accompanied by Hugh J. Cannon, embarked on a world tour of missions of the Church, a tour that would take them away from their homes for more than a year. In the diary he kept of this historic tour, President McKay wrote the following concerning his departure from home.*

*Saturday, December 4, 1920.* A telephone call at 6:30 A.M. from my Scottish friend and brother, William Kenly, who just wanted to say goodbye, started me out with the full realization that this would be my last day with my loved ones for perhaps eight or ten months—probably longer. As the morning hours lengthened into day, this realization became more intense and my feelings more tender. The press of packing and attending to a hundred eleventh-hour duties proved to be a good channel into which my thoughts and feelings were diverted. However, it was not so with Ray [Sister McKay]. It was plainly evident that she, bless her heroic soul, was making a brave struggle to keep back the tears. She reminded me of one of the pretty little geysers in Yellowstone—it would remain placid and peaceful for a while, but soon the forces, hidden and turbulent, would stir the surface of the water until it swelled, bubbled, and boiled over the rim and the pent-up forces were set free. I hope the tears that bedimmed Ray's eyes so frequently during the day proved a relief to the rising emotion she so heroically tried to subdue.

Parting from those we love is never an easy task, but today it seemed more difficult than ever. Every little household duty when performed seemed to say, "This is the last time for awhile." Even the fire in the furnace looked gloomy when I threw in the last shovelful of coal.

However, I kept my feelings pretty well under control until I began to say goodbye to the children. Baby, thinking I was going to coo to him, looked up and gave me his sweetest smile. The beautiful, innocent radiance of his baby face will be a treasured memory all during my missionary tour.

Then came Ned, my affectionate, tender boy. He couldn't realize why his daddy was sobbing. His tear-dimmed eyes and inquiring expression revealed the emotion in his little soul. What a blessing that it would be but transient in his childish nature!

The parting moment with my sweetheart and true, devoted wife, my life's companion and joy, I cannot describe. Such sacred scenes are not for expression in words—they find expression only in the depths of a loving soul.

Emma Rae, Lou Jean, and Llewelyn accompanied me to the train—Emma Rae, the "Sunbeam"; Lou Jean, the "Rosebud"; and Llewelyn, the "Leader," who in his young manhood, in the absence of his brother and father, must assume all the duties of the farm and household heretofore carried by the three of us. No father can be prouder of his children than I, nor more confident of their fidelity and desire for success. Parting from them at the station stirred my feelings wholly beyond control. I left them, though, having the comforting assurance that each would be a sweetheart to Mama and live for her comfort and pleasure.

# China Dedicated for the Preaching of the Gospel

*In his world tour diary under date of January 9, 1921, President McKay gives the following account of the dedication of the Chinese realm.*

Elder Hugh J. Cannon and I have traveled continuously since last Tuesday with the sole purpose in mind to be here in Peking on this Sabbath day.

Before we left home, President Grant suggested that when we were in China, if we felt so impressed, we were to set the land apart for the preaching of the gospel. As Peking is really the heart of China, we had concluded that this would be an appropriate place to perform this sacred and far-reaching duty.

The sky was cloudless. The sun's bright rays tempered the winter air to pleasantness. Every impression following our earnest prayers together and in secret seemed to confirm our conclusions arrived at last evening; viz., that it seems that the time is near at hand when these teeming millions should at least be given a glimpse of the glorious light now shining among the children of men in other and more advanced nations.

Accordingly, we strolled almost aimlessly, wondering where it would be possible to find a secluded spot for worship and prayer. We entered that part of the imperial city, known as the Forbidden City, and walked by the famous old buildings formerly used as temples. On we walked until we came to a small grove of cypress trees on the edge of what appeared to have been an old moat running parallel with one of the walls. As we proceeded from east to west, we passed a tree with a large branch shooting out on the north side, and I distinctly received the prompting to choose that as the spot. However, we passed it and walked to the west end but returned again to the designated tree, realizing it to be the most suitable place in the grove.

Under the century-old limbs and green leaves of this, one of God's own temples, with uncovered heads, we supplicated our Father in heaven and by the authority of the Holy Melchizedek Priesthood, and in the name of the Only Begotten of the Father, turned the key that unlocked the door for the entrance into this benighted and famine-stricken land of the authorized servants of God to preach the true and restored gospel of Jesus Christ.

Brother Cannon, with well-chosen words and with a spirit of deep earnestness and humility, blessed the chosen spot as one of prayer and supplication to the Almighty. It was plainly evident that he was sincerely affected by the solemnity of the occasion.

Acting under appointment of the prophet, seer, and revelator, and by virtue of the holy apostleship, I then dedicated and set apart the Chinese realm for the preaching of the glad tidings of great joy as revealed in this dispensation through the Prophet Joseph Smith, and prayed particularly that the present government may become stabilized, if not by the Chinese themselves, then by the intervention of the civilized powers of the world.

*Brother Cannon, in an article published in* The Improvement Era, *Vol. 24, pages 443-46, 1920-21, gives the following interesting account of this dedication within the walls of the Forbidden City, Peking, China.*

Elder David O. McKay, of the Council of the Twelve, and the writer, arrived in Peking, the chief city of China, Saturday evening, January 8, 1921. The horde of ragged mendicants, grimy porters and insistent jinrikisha men, who fought noisily for possession of us as we emerged from the station, was not such as to inspire a feeling of affectionate brotherhood. However, we had gone to Peking to do the Lord's will, as nearly as we could ascertain what it was. His inspiration rested upon his servant in charge, and Elder McKay decided that the land should be dedicated and set apart for the preaching of the gospel of the Master.

It seemed most desirable that this should be done on the following day, as that was the only Sabbath we should be in Peking. But where, in the mist of that clamor and confusion, could a suitable spot be found? The city lies on a level, barren plain. There are no forests, and so far as we knew, no groves nor even clumps of tress. We were wholly unfamiliar with the city and had met no one who could enlighten us. If we went outside the surrounding walls, there was reason to believe no secluded spot could be found nor the ever-present crowd of supplicants avoided.

January 9 dawned clear and cold. With no definite goal in mind, we left the hotel and walked through the legation quarter, under the shadow of dear Old Glory, out into what is known as "The Forbidden City," past the crumbling temples reared to an "Unknown God." Directed, as we believe, by a Higher Power, we came to a grove of cypress trees, partially surrounded by a moat, and walked to its extreme northwest corner, then retraced our steps until we reached a tree with divided trunk which had attracted our attention when we first saw it.

"This is the spot," said Elder McKay.

A reposeful peace hovered over the place which seemed already hallowed; one felt it was almost a profanation to tread thereon with covered head and feet.

Two men were in sight, but they seemed oblivious to our presence, and they soon left the grove. There, in the heart of a city with a million inhabitants, we were entirely alone, except for the presence of a divinely sweet and comforting Spirit.

An act destined to affect the lives of four hundred and fifty millions of people now living, as of millions and perhaps billions yet unborn, calls forth feelings of profound solemnity, and that, too, despite the fact that the vast majority of those affected may die in ignorance of the event.

After a prayer had been offered and the spot dedicated as the place of supplication and for the fulfillment of the object of our visit, Elder David O. McKay, in the authority of the holy apostleship, dedicated and set apart the Chinese realm for the preaching of the gospel of the Lord Jesus Christ, whenever the Church Authorities shall deem it advisable to send out missionaries for that purpose. Never was the power of his calling more apparent in his utterances. He blessed the land and its benighted people and supplicated the Almighty to acknowledge this blessing. He prayed that famine and pestilence might be stayed, and that the government might become stable, either through its own initiative, or by the intervention of other powers, and that superstition and error, which for ages have enveloped the people, might be discarded, and truth take their place. He supplicated the Lord to send to this land broadminded and intelligent men and women, that upon them might rest the spirit of discernment and the power to comprehend the Chinese nature, so that in the souls of this people an appreciation of the glorious gospel might be awakened.

It was such a prayer and blessing as must be recognized in

heaven, and though the effects may not be suddenly apparent, they will be nonetheless real.

If this nation would observe one of the simplest of the Lord's commandments, that of the monthly fast, and give the meals thus saved to those in need, the famine problem would be solved. This would furnish two meals to each of the fifteen million sufferers.

The cypress tree is a symbol of sorrow and sadness in China, and this cypress grove seemed a peculiarly fitting place in which to invoke the blessing of heaven upon this oppressed and sorrowing people.

At Shanhaikwan, the point at which that wonder of wonders, the great Chinese wall meets the sea, and on the frontier of the famine district, we took a picture. Though the morning was bitterly cold, we judged it to be zero weather, some of these people were nearly naked. The shreds of patches which only partially covered their emaciated and shivering bodies might well feel complimented at being called rags.

One contemplates China's past accomplishments with a feeling akin to awe. We respect old age, and especially so when, with antiquity, we see achievement; and it is well to remember that this land had a highly developed civilization nearly twenty-five centuries before the Christian era.

Notwithstanding her present pitiably inane condition, we have met some admirable Chinese people and cherish the sincere hope that at no very distant day the light of the gospel may penetrate the present overwhelming darkness. Though the abject misery we beheld appealed to our tenderest sympathies, gold and silver we could not give, but the door was unlocked for them through which they may enter into eternal life.

# On the Rim of a Volcanic Crater

*Following a most inspirational meeting at Hilo, Hawaii, President McKay recorded in his world tour diary on February 10, 1921, the following incident of a trip to "Kilauea," the largest active volcano in the world.*

It was eleven o'clock P.M. when nine of us in two automobiles left Hilo for a thirty-seven-mile drive to the crater. The entire distance, the roadway is lined with *ohia* trees, ferns, and the *lehua,* the island flower. As the headlight flashed on this tropical foliage and brought out in bold relief the beautiful flowers in full bloom, I thought I had never before taken a night ride to equal this midnight auto drive.

When yet within six miles or more of the volcano, we could see its lurid light shooting up toward the clear sky. Unfortunately, just at the rim of the crater, which, by the way, is about ten miles in circumference, one of our autos balked—David Kalani's; but we drove the distance twice, and thus all nine of us arrived without much delay.

After going as near as possible with the autos, we began our ascent to the steam-cauldron that was filling the air with sulphurous vapor.

The first distinct sound I heard was like a blacksmith's bellows raised to the nth power. Then, as we ascended the top of the crater, what I beheld will never be forgotten. Rivers of molten lava flowing in a sea of fire and brimstone, bubbling and spurting from 10,000 cauldrons. A miniature volcano just below us blowing an acetylene flame, with the noise of a thousand blowers, and shooting red hot lava sparks a hundred feet in the air! Grotesquely shaped animal-like figures projecting from the sides of the crater. Dinosaurs and plesiosaurs, half-hidden by the smoky vapors that arose from everywhere and floated out into the blackness of the night toward the top of Mauna Loa. Great, black, whale-like spots floating and writhing on top of the lurid red surface of the fiery furnace, until a burst of gases dissipated it into a dozen shattered remnants. A molten stream flowing to the right, another flowing to the left in the same lake, each seemingly stirred by a thousand demons, urging it to the onslaught. When these two forces met, there was seething and spurting, twisting and writhing; then they sank to some underground cavern flamed once again with the fires of Hades.

But it is vain to attempt to describe the indescribable or to picture the unpicturable. Kilauea to be appreciated or abhorred must be seen in nature's setting, not puny man's.

We arrived at the crater's edge at two A.M. and walked around over the sharp and broken lava, watched the ever-changing surface of the cauldron, or dozed upon the rocks until sunrise of Friday, February 11, 1921.

Brother Cannon, Brother Smith, Sister Budd, Elders Cox, Davis, Swain, David Kalani, and I then stood on the brink while the Kodaks clicked, after which we returned to Hilo, enjoying the morning ride, notwithstanding the sleepless night.

*During this eventful night, members of the party were witnesses to an inspirational event. Sister Virginia Budd (Jacobsen), a member of the party, who at the time was serving as a missionary in Hawaii, has written the following account of what took place on that occasion.*

The question is often asked, "Do we really have revelation today?" A very impressive incident which happened while I was filling a mission in Hawaii is an answer to this question, and is told with the permission of President David O. McKay, since it concerns him.

It happened in 1921, while President McKay and Elder Hugh Cannon were making a tour of the missions of the world. After a day of inspiring conference meetings in Hilo, Hawaii, a night trip to the Kilauea volcano was arranged for the visiting brethren and some of the missionaries. About nine o'clock that evening, two carloads, about ten of us, took off for the then very active volcano.

We stood on the rim of that fiery pit watching Pele in her satanic antics, our backs chilled by the cold winds sweeping down from snowcapped Mauna Loa, and our faces almost blistered by the heat of the molten lava. Tiring of the cold, one of the elders discovered a volcanic balcony about four feet down inside the crater where observers could watch the display without being chilled by the wind. It seemed perfectly sound, and the railing on the open side of it formed a fine protection from the intense heat, making it an excellent place to view the spectacular display.

After first testing its safety, Brother McKay and three of the elders climbed down into the hanging balcony. As they stood there warm and comfortable, they teased the others of us more timid ones who had hesitated to take advantage of the protection they had found. For quite some time we all watched the ever-changing sight as we alternately chilled and roasted.

After being down there in their protected spot for some time, suddenly Brother McKay said to those with him, "Brethren, I feel impressed that we should get out of here."

With that he assisted the elders to climb out, and then they in turn helped him up to the wind-swept rim. It seems incredible, but almost immediately the whole balcony crumbled and fell with a roar into the molten lava a hundred feet or so below.

It is easy to visualize the feelings of those who witnessed this terrifying experience. Not a word was said . . . the whole thing was too awful, with all that word means. The only sound was the hiss and roar of Pele, the Fire Goddess of old Hawaii, screaming her disappointment.

None of us who were witnesses to this experience could ever doubt the reality of revelation in our day. Some might say it was merely inspiration, but to us, it was a direct revelation given to a worthy man.

# Gift of Interpretation of Tongues

One of the most important events on my world tour of the missions of the Church was the gift of interpretation of the English tongue to the Saints of New Zealand at a session of their conference, held on the 23rd day of April, 1921, at Puke Tapu

Branch, Waikato District, Huntly, New Zealand.

The service was held in a large tent, beneath the shade of which hundreds of earnest men and women gathered in anxious anticipation of seeing and hearing an apostle of the Church, the first one to visit that land.

When I looked over that vast assemblage and contemplated the great expectations that filled the hearts of all who had met together, I realized how inadequately I might satisfy the ardent desires of their souls, and I yearned, most earnestly, for the gift of tongues that I might be able to speak to them in their native language.

Until that moment I had not given much serious thought to the gift of tongues, but on that occasion, I wished with all my heart that I might be worthy of that divine power.

In other missions I had spoken through an interpreter but, able as all interpreters are, I nevertheless felt hampered—in fact, somewhat inhibited—in presenting my message.

Now I faced an audience that had assembled with unusual expectations, and I realized, as never before, the great responsibility of my office. From the depth of my soul, I prayed for divine assistance.

When I arose to give my address, I said to Brother Stuart Meha, our interpreter, that I would speak without his translating, sentence by sentence, what I said. Then to the audience I continued:

"I wish, oh, how I wish I had the power to speak to you in your own tongue, that I might tell you what is in my heart; but since I have not the gift, I pray, and I ask you to pray, that you might have the spirit of interpretation, of discernment, that you may understand at least the spirit while I am speaking, and then you will get the words and the thought when Brother Meha interprets."

My sermon lasted forty minutes, and I have never addressed a more attentive, a more respectful audience. My listeners were in perfect rapport—this I knew when I saw tears in their eyes. Some of them at least, perhaps most of them, who did not understand English, had the gift of interpretation.

Brother Sidney Christy, a native New Zealander who had been

a student at Brigham Young University, at the close of my address whispered to me, "Brother McKay, they got your message!"

"Yes," I replied, "I think so, but for the benefit of some who may not have understood, we shall have Brother Meha give a synopsis of it in Maori."

During the translation, some of the Maoris corrected him on some points, showing that they had a clear conception of what had been said in English.

Two subsequent experiences, one of which occurred on that memorable world tour, enabled me to realize more clearly how the spirit of interpretation may come.

On one occasion when I was addressing an audience at Aintab, Syria, I realized that Elder J. Wilford Booth, who was translating into the Turkish language, had interpreted incorrectly a thought I had expressed and, although I did not then—and do not now—understand a word of Turkish, I stopped Brother Booth in his translation and said, "That was the wrong interpretation, Brother Booth." I then repeated my sentence.

"How did you know, Brother McKay?" he asked. "I gave the opposite meaning."

Later, when I was called to preside over the European Mission, I was one day addressing an audience at Rotterdam. Brother Cornelius Zappey was interpreting, and, on that occasion, I had an experience identical to that which occurred with Brother Booth. When I called Brother Zappey's attention to what I felt was not the correct interpretation, he laughingly said to the audience, before making the correction, "There is no need of my interpreting. Brother McKay understands Dutch."

I cite these two incidents merely to emphasize the fact that, although I did not realize when I was in New Zealand how the spirit of interpretation operated on others, yet I accepted it as a fact, as a truth, that later was demonstrated to me by the Spirit of the Lord.

Another lesson that these incidents have taught me is this: that none of us should be too prone to condemn things which we do not fully understand.

"For what man knoweth the things of man, save the spirit of man which is in him? even so the things of God knoweth no man, but the Spirit of God." (1 Cor. 2:11.)

My experience has taught me that the safe anchor of the soul, and indeed, the security and happiness in life are founded upon a faith in God, upon a faith in the divinity of Jesus Christ and in his gospel of peace and life, upon a faith in the efficacy of prayer and in the power of the priesthood as bestowed upon the Prophet Joseph Smith and through him conferred upon others who have been and are worthy to receive this blessed possession.

Such a faith becomes as fixed and constant in its guidance as the Polar Star. It enables one to overcome trials and discouragements, to face life with courage, to meet disaster with fortitude, and, when the final event comes, to face death without fear.

*NOTE: In the Church Historian's office, in Blue Book 4,081 . 6-8935, following an account of the gift of interpretation of the English tongue to the Saints of New Zealand, are testimonies as to the actuality of the occurrence by Wi Smith, Sidney Christy, Stuart Meha, and Karena W. Takoro. These testimonies were prepared in 1934 at the request of President Rufus K. Hardy. Original, handwritten letters from natives who were present on this occasion, testifying that they received the gift of interpretation while President McKay was speaking, are also preserved in President McKay's scrapbooks.*

*Of this inspirational event, Brother Wi Smith, in a letter dated May 14, 1934, said:*

This is to certify that I, Wi Smith, president of the Mahia District, do hereby state and declare that, at the Mormon *Hui Tau* held at Huntly on April 23, 1921, I did personally witness and hear Apostle David O. McKay offer up a prayer asking the Lord to enlighten the Maori congregation during his sermon without the help of a Maori interpreter.

And I testify that this eventually happened; all the Maoris young and old enjoyed his sermon.

*Brother Sidney Christy, in a letter dated May 18, 1934, wrote:*

At the opening session of this conference (*Hui Tau*, April 23, 1921), Apostle David O. McKay was one of the speakers. He opened his speech by saying, "Although I know there are two very competent interpreters present in Brother Sidney Christy and

Brother Stewart Meha, I pray that the Spirit which emanates from our Heavenly Father may permeate throughout this gathering so that whatever I say may be understood by everyone present without the aid of an interpreter.".

Here, I, Sidney Christy, do testify that after he had spoken but a few minutes the apostle had the whole congregation in tears, and when the old Maori people who did not understand English were approached after the service, they stated that they knew every word uttered by the apostle.

During this conference there were two Josephites who were doing their level best to make trouble. After one of the meetings in which they interrupted the speakers several times, one of them approached Elder McKay, and in a sarcastic manner said to him, "I would like to shake hands with an apostle of The Church of Jesus Christ of Latter-day Saints, for I have never seen one before." He then extended his hand, and as soon as it came in contact with the apostle's, he shivered with an ague and collapsed at the apostle's feet and sobbed. The apostle thereupon lifted him up by the hand and said, "Brother, let me give you some advice: Never tear another man's house down. If you wish to use a hammer, use it in building a house of your own." The other Josephite then came and took his friend away.

This was witnessed by scores of people, and it is common knowledge throughout the New Zealand Mission.

# The Lord's Help in Time of Need

*Taken from President McKay's world tour diary written April 24, 1921, at Huntly, New Zealand.*

Sunday Morning, April 24, 1921, dawned in a cloudless east and promised a clear day.

We held the usual prayers and scripture-repeating exercises, and at 10 A.M. met in the Sunday School session of conference.

Having wet my feet yesterday, I have aggravated my cold. As a result, I'm so hoarse I can scarcely speak above a whisper, a condition that forebodes difficulty and disappointment for me and for the people on this the heaviest day of our tour.

10 A.M. I managed to tell the children a story, but my voice was weak and husky. However, Brother Cannon was at his best, so we had a excellent meeting.

A thousand people—Maoris and Pakehas, sitting, reclining, and standing—assembled for the afternoon service. They came with curiosity and high expectations. It was my duty to give them a message, but I was not only too hoarse to speak and be heard by that crowd, but I was also ill.

However, with a most appealing prayer in my heart for divine help and guidance, I arose to perform my duty. My voice was tight and husky. Five minutes after I began, someone shouted from the group standing on my right, "Joseph Smith didn't receive the revelation on polygamy!"

Evidently the emissaries of the devil had chosen an opportune moment to obtain some free advertising. I hesitated a moment, turned my head in his direction, and saw some men scuffling and the crowd beginning to sway toward them. Motioning to the audience to remain quiet, I said, with as much good nature as I could muster, "When the sons of God met, the devil came also." Many grasped the application and broke into laughter. Some began to clap, but I motioned for order and continued with my discourse.

Then happened what had never before happened to me. I entered into my theme with all the earnestness and vehemence I could command and spoke as loud as possible. Feeling my voice getting clearer and more resonant, I soon forgot I had a voice and thought only of the truth I wanted my hearers to understand and accept. For forty minutes I continued with my address, and when I concluded, my voice was as resonant and clear as it ever was.

Brother Cannon concluded with a fervent testimony; and thus our fifth meeting closed with thanksgiving and rejoicing in every heart.

When I told Brother Cannon and some other brethren how

earnestly I had prayed for the very blessing I had received, he said, "I too, was praying—never prayed more fervently for a speaker in my life."

# A Beautiful Vision

*Written on May 10, 1921, as Elder McKay and Brother Cannon approached Apia, Samoa.*

On Tuesday, May 10, 1921, we sailed all day on the smoothest sea of our entire trip. The slightly undulating waves had been so free from even signs of unrest that the slight ripples discernible appeared on the surface like millions of little squares—like plaited cloth with the rich design of the same deep blue material as the body.

Nearing Savaii, we could see with the aid of field glasses the "Spouting Horns," which looked like geysers. On our right we caught a glimpse of the little village nestling safely in the mouth of an extinct valcano on the little island of Apolima.

Toward evening, the reflection of the afterglow of a beautiful sunset was most splendid! The sky was tinged with pink, and the clouds lingering around the horizon were fringed with various hues of crimson and orange, while the heavy cloud farther to the west was somber purple and black. These colors cast varying shadows on the peaceful surface of the water. Those from the cloud were long and dark, those from the crimson-tinged sky, clear but rose-tinted and fading into a faint pink that merged into the clear blue of the ocean. Gradually, the shadows became deeper and heavier, and then all merged into a beautiful calm twilight that made the sea look like a great mirror upon which fell the faint light of the crescent moon.

Pondering still upon this beautiful scene, I lay in my berth at ten o'clock that night and thought to myself: Charming as it is, it doesn't stir my soul with emotion as do the innocent lives of children, and the sublime characters of loved ones and friends. Their beauty, unselfishness, and heroism are after all the most glorious!

I then fell asleep, and beheld in vision something infinitely sublime. In the distance I beheld a beautiful white city. Though it was far away, yet I seemed to realize that trees with luscious fruit, shrubbery with gorgeously tinted leaves, and flowers in perfect bloom abounded everywhere. The clear sky above seemed to reflect these beautiful shades of color. I then saw a great concourse of people approaching the city. Each one wore a white flowing robe and a white headdress. Instantly my attention seemed centered upon their leader, and though I could see only the profile of his features and his body, I recognized him at once as my Savior! The tint and radiance of his countenance were glorious to behold. There was a peace about him which seemed sublime—it was divine!

The city, I understood, was his. It was the City Eternal; and the people following him were to abide there in peace and eternal happiness.

But who were they?

As if the Savior read my thoughts, he answered by pointing to a semicircle that then appeared above them, and on which were written in gold the words:

> *These Are They Who Have Overcome the World—*
> *Who Have Truly Been Born Again!*

When I awoke, it was breaking day over Apia harbor.

# A Memorable Visit to Samoa

*Among the sacred and never-to-be-forgotten incidents experienced by President McKay during his tour was that of the singular and soul-stirring farewell to the Saints and friends of the islands of Samoa, which took place at Sauniatu, Samoa, May 31, 1921.*

*Elder John Q. Adams, who at the time was the president of the Samoan Mission, gives the following vivid word picture of events leading up to this incident.*

Samoa's big day, for months heralded and anticipated by Saint and stranger alike, the day when for the first time since the dawn of human life in the isles, a real, live apostle was to set foot upon these tropic shores, is fast drawing to an all-too-rapid conclusion, for the hours of such occasions race by on the wings of moments.

We had scarcely one week after the receipt of Brother McKay's wireless from New Zealand in which to scatter the news about Upolu and Savaii, and two British islands upon which he and Brother Cannon were first to land. In Upolu this was not a difficult feat, as there are fair trails, and our headquarters are on this island, so we had couriers going to the two ends the day the word came. Getting to Savaii might ordinarily have been quite a proposition on such short notice, but not in this case, for the Lord came to the rescue, and we learned of a boat going to Palauli, the very place we had hoped to reach early the next morning. Not trusting to mail, we had a Samoan missionary make a special trip. Within two hours after he landed there, so he afterward said, a messenger had been sent and reached the conference president a dozen miles down the rough trail, and that night away went one elder one way, and another left down the opposite side of the island, a distance of two hundred miles staring them in the face, and a whole island to notify. So went news in olden time before the age of more perfect communication, and so went our heralds, for Samoa is yet primitive in her outer isles.

On the morning of May 10 definite word came from the S. S. *Tofua* by wireless that she would make Apia in the early evening. Choir practice in the Pesega Church was on, a council circle of church chiefs sat across the way on Apia's big house considering problems of the near arrival, and we missionaries were kneeling at early evening prayer, when a breathless messenger spread consternation in our midst with the announcement that the S. S. *Tofua* was in port. The hurry and scurry of the succeeding few minutes may only partly be imagined. Suffice it to add that all the Saints, including the band, chiefs, schools, and members in general were at the wharf within half an hour. At the request of the Saints that Elders McKay and Cannon remain aboard ship until morning in order that a fitting reception, the fruits of months of preparation, be accorded, Elder McKay graciously acceded to President Adams and a number of elders who went out to the ship anchored in the bay for that purpose.

At nine o'clock on the eleventh President and Sister Adams

and Elder and Sister Griffiths went out to the ship in two great long rowboats all decorated with garlands of vines and flowers, and the apostle and his companions were escorted back to the wharf. One of the crews rowed with the old-fashioned paddles used in native canoes, and as they paddled joyously along to the accompaniment of typical Samoan boat songs, punctuated by occasional yells of accentuation, it pleased them immensely to have Brother McKay join in their whoops in sheer boyish glee.

As soon as greetings with the dozen and a half elders were over with, the British custom officials courteously dispensed with regulations in which they are invariably strict and allowed us to go directly to the throng who were awaiting us in front of the building. Grouped separately were the chiefs, missionaries, Relief Societies, schools, and band, with many strangers, interested onlookers. They had all heard often in sermons and otherwise for years of the existence of prophets and apostles nowadays as formerly, and now was come their opportunity to see a real one. All work of government employees at the waterfront stopped for the same reason. From group to group went Brother McKay and Elder Cannon, greeting warmly the various persons and in turn receiving veritable homage and reverence. The spirit on this occasion was wonderful.

Then all formed in line, and down Apia's one thoroughfare went the procession headed by the famous Mormon band from Sauniatu. After them came a car or so and then the schools and missionaries and others. At the doors of all business establishments persons crowded. Business was at a standstill.

Perhaps thirty high chiefs, in the Church and out of it, entertained in an august council circle in which the usual eloquent Samoan welcoming speeches were delivered and replied to by the visitors, and the proverbial bowl of *kava* or native drink of respect passed with becoming ceremony and dignity. As a distinct mark of respect, Brother McKay was presented with one of the largest pieces of *kava* root ever seen in these parts to take home as a keepsake.

At three P.M., a great feast, spread under a coconut leaf canopy, was partaken of by hundreds. At this, as well as at the events of the remainder of the day, were many of the highest officials and chiefs of the government and of the islands. It was a day to be remembered, and a historical one for Samoa in general, and our church here in particular.

The next four days were filled with conference meetings. At times there were as many as 1,510 persons present at the meetings and on the lawns surrounding the scene of action. At these sessions President McKay and Brother Cannon occupied most of the time, and the spiritual feasts were memorable ones.

Frequently there would be many in the audience weeping, and we knew that some of them could not understand English, in which language the talks were first given and then interpreted by Su'a Kippen. The Holy Spirit was so strong and convincing that before the Samoan translation had been given, tears were shed, and the principles discussed were all applicable to the occasion and the needs of the islands.

During the week baptismal services were held, a missionary testimony meeting was held, and a concert by the Sauniatu band and school presented. All in all, the week was a perfect success from every standpoint and will ever stand out in mind as one of the rare occasions of life, and as for the work here in the islands it may well be justly considered a historical event, for never before had any General Authority been in Samoa. The warm welcome of the outside chiefs, a very remarkable transformation of the bitter sentiment of bygone years, was no inconsiderable element of contributary satisfaction.

*Visits were made to Pago Pago and to Tutuila under very trying circumstances in a small gasoline boat. Elders McKay and Cannon also took a twelve-mile walk up the coast from Pago Pago to Mapusaga, where a Church school is located.*

On this occasion, and at frequent other times, they were forced to undergo what we more experienced people in island conditions would call real privations, yet they held up splendidly without complaint, with no serious after-affects, which is a source of wonder, for they are not acclimated, are not as young as the elders who ordinarily rough it here, and are not used to the native food, of which they have eaten quite freely. The Lord's blessings are with them in a physical way, as he is spiritually, and despite the strenuous experiences that no doubt await them in the coming months, when they will have been in all climes from torrid to frigid, they will assuredly be taken care of by our Heavenly Father. This much we feel we should say at this particular point in our narrative, for they have had some exertions since landing here—in fact, it has pretty well been one continuous period of action.

We might go on and on and still have quite sufficient material left to compose many a page of description of this most wonderful of visits during the past three weeks spent in the company of Elders McKay and Cannon, in which their inspiring discourses and daily walk and talk have been of a character and faith-building nature; and we might also go to tempting and disproportionate lengths as to the part played by Samoa and her Saints and people at large in all the multitude of activities, but we shall close with the briefest of reference to a most magnificent example of the attitude of the Saints and people toward our brethren and how it has been regarded, namely, the farewell that Sauniatu spontaneously provided.

One of the noteworthy features of the whole visit has been the great number of sick and afflicted that came or were brought to them for administration. We had been busy all morning with the brethren inspecting the school at Sauniatu, one of the most important phases of their visit, in which Brother McKay declared to the children that from now on Sauniatu would be numbered among the schools of the Church system of education. From there we repaired to the mission home and administered to a number of sick, at the conclusion of which we stepped out into the front room ready to spring into the saddle for the return. But no! The good Saints of the village had a farewell handshake to claim. The Relief Society sisters were lined across the room in a double column, and on out onto the porch and around to one side the lines stretched. The plaintive farewell song *"Tofa, My Feleni"* was struck up and from one to the other we went with warm handclasps and fervent words. Tears were in evidence from the beginning.

*Of this touching farewell, President McKay has recorded the following in his personal diary, dated May 31, 1921.*

Following the *Alofa* and the presentation of the *Au Tonga* to Brother Hugh J. Cannon and me, the fathers and mothers came for blessings for themselves as well as for their children, and we received them all even up to an hour past the appointed time to leave. Healthy, robust babies, as well as those who were ill and threatened with blindness, were blessed as sincerely and prayerfully as our souls could bless.

As we came out of our room, we found the people standing in double column from our door out across the lawn to the street, the mothers nearest, then the fathers, and last the youth and children.

They had been informed that we should not have time to shake their hands, so they had prepared a farewell song for the occasion. This they began to sing as we came out. Brother and Sister Adams led, followed by Brother Cannon, and I came last, shaking hands with everyone. When those kindhearted sisters began to kiss my hand and cry, I felt a pretty tender feeling take possession of me, which was well defined when their sobbing interrupted their singing.

When at length I came to old Brother Sai Masina, whose one last wish, as he had said, had now been gratified, I put my arms around him and let the tears spring to my eyes as he sobbed against my breast. By this time the entire assembly was in tears. Staunch old Opapo, the head man of the village, sobbed like a child, and clung to us as though we were his sons. Kippen, too, threw himself on my neck and cried aloud.

Finally the last little boys crowding around had pressed our hands, so with tear-bedimmed eyes we walked slowly toward the stream beyond which our horses were waiting. The band on the porch played "*Tofa, My Feleni*," and the people stood waving their fond farewell. As a turn in the road obstructed them from view, I thought I had seldom experienced a more impressive farewell.

Just as we had mounted our horses, we looked toward the turn at the bridge and saw the crowd, headed by the band, coming toward us. Before we were ready to start, they gathered around us again, eager to have one more handshake. It was touching indeed to see the old patriarch Sai Masina crowd his way through to reach my outstretched hand.

From that spot to the dugway leading down to the ocean, there is a straight, grassy roadway, lined with tall native trees and tropical vines. As we rode slowly up the gentle incline, the band leading, the people followed as if they just would not or could not yield to parting. We had gained perhaps a quarter of a mile ahead of them, when I felt impressed to say, "I think we should return and leave our blessing with them here in this beautiful grove."

"I think that's inspiration," said Brother Adams.

As we approached the sobbing crowd, I could not help thrilling with the picturesqueness of the scene. The green avenue, lined with stately trees whose intertwining branches formed a vista ending only at the village, the white dresses of the women, and the red turban of the band boys' uniforms stood out in beautiful contrast to the various shades of green surrounding them. It was a setting and an occasion worthy of the best efforts of the most gifted artist.

Hanging my folded umbrella on an overhanging limb, I dismounted, and Kippen told them why we had come back. Their sobs were louder than my voice when I began the prayer, but they became more subdued as I continued and their *"Amene"* was distinct and impressive at the close.

At this point I shall record what happened later in the day, but which was not reported to us until the arrival of two of the elders on the following afternoon. After they had watched us until we were beyond their sight, they returned solemnly to the village and separated to their huts. Kippen, who had been our interpreter, immediately sat down and wrote the prayer as he remembered it. He and some others then conceived the idea of burying a copy of it on the spot where I had stood and erecting a pile of stones as a marking place. The suggestion, it seems, was no sooner made than acted upon. The town bell was rung, the people assembled, the plan was presented and approved, and the crowd once more walked to the place of parting.

Here the prayer was read, a hole dug, and the bottle in which a copy had been sealed, together with an account of the entire proceedings, buried beneath a pile of stones, each of the heads of families throwing a handful or two of soil to assist in the covering. The branch on which my umbrella had been hung was taken to the village to be kept as a souvenir, and steps were taken to erect a small monument of what seemed to them and to us to be a sacred spot.

David O. McKay Monument at Sauniatu, Samoa, dedicated May 31, 1922. It was erected in commemoration of the apostolic blessing of Elder McKay on May 31, 1921.

Though it began to rain just as we left the conference house, it stopped within two minutes, and we rode the twenty miles to Pesega without getting wet. This was truly significant, for it rained hard during the afternoon at Sauniatu and *poured* at Pesega. Fifteen minutes after we entered the mission house, it rained in good old torrential fashion.

We retired feeling happy and thankful for the associations and experiences of one of the most memorable days of our tour, indeed of our lives. "Oh, I never will forget you, Samoa *e le galo atu.*"

*Elder Adams, in his report of this event on May 31, 1921, said:*

Thither had followed the weeping throng of Saints, reluctant to sever the intimate and affectionate association of the immediate past. Still on and on they traversed the beautiful tropical trail that bisects the adjacent rubber plantation for a mile, a reverent group of two hundred, headed by the band, to whose strains of the pathetic native farewell melody "Good-bye, my *Feleni,*" they slowly and solemnly marched. Elder McKay far in advance, with his party of four horsemen, looking back with tears in his eyes, could bear it no longer—the scene and the spirit and influence of it all were altogether too affecting and remarkable. In shaking voice he bade us return with him for the third ordeal of the final farewell, a moment and an occasion of a lifetime or of centuries.

There the now silent and expectant groups were standing disconsolate as Israel of old bereft of their Moses. He dismounted in the trail, and raising aloft his hands as a patriarch of the past, he pronounced a remarkable and soul-stirring benediction, all clear and now partly fulfilled.

It is the testimony of some who cast their eyes upward momentarily as inspired words flowed in great power from Elder McKay's lips that a halo of brightness rested upon him like a shaft of white light, and certain it is that the borderland of heaven and earth rested in close proximity to the spot where was given this wonderful manifestation and blessing. Each listener's soul throbbed with the conviction of the truth.

Immediately after the final farewell, we left the meditating group of Saints still standing silent in the foreground, stunned at eventually losing sight of the receding figures, albeit in apparent enthrallment. We afterward learned that they at once set about perpetuating the day's great event. A hole was dug at the exact spot where had stood Brother McKay when blessing them, and into this was consigned a hermetically sealed bottle, containing a record of the occasion, including a copy of the prayer as well as Kippen Su'a could recollect it there and then. Hymns were sung, discourses delivered, and explanations again made in detail of the significance of the great day.

Several other events have occurred since, but we shall say nothing of any of these, for they all sink into insignificance before the simple splendor and ineffaceable recollection of that sacred hour on that trail when the hearts of a whole village became as one in throbbing to the inspiration of a single thought and hope—the full realization by a whole-souled race that they had been favored by an apostolic visit and could only reciprocate by revealing the appreciation and gratitude with which their great warm souls glowed.

A year later, on May 31, 1922, one could have glimpsed a similar scene reenacted, only on a larger scale. On that day a monument was unveiled and dedicated. It was erected in commemoration of the visit of Elders David O. McKay and Hugh J. Cannon and of the remarkable parting benediction uttered on the spot by Elder McKay. The monument measures six feet square at the base and is thirteen feet high. On the face of the four-foot square section of the shaft is a beautiful bronze plate, twelve by thirty inches in dimension, on which is etched in conspicuous lettering the following legend of the visit:

> *Today, Tuesday, May 31, 1921*
> *Apostle David O. McKay Stood Just Across the River*
> *And Pronounced a Memorable Apostolic Blessing*
> *Upon the Assembled Sauniatu Saints*
> *A Fitting Climax to a Perfect Visit*
> *Samoa's Love Is Told Thus Mizpa*
> *O Le Faailoga Lenci O Le Alofa*
> *Atoatoa O Samoa Mo Misi Makei Ma*
> *Misi Kanona. Mesepa.*

The dedicatory exercises, attended by hundreds of people,

dressed in white, and by forty missionaries, consisted of a very impressive and appropriate program of songs, speeches, the dedicatory prayer by President John Q. Adams, and music by a new brass band of thirty pieces, known as "Brother McKay's Brass Band." As the shaft was unveiled, the band broke out with the national anthem, and up stepped scores of school children, dressed in white, with armfuls of wreaths and bouquets of tropical flowers, fairly burying the base of the structure with the fragrance and the riot of color of the islands. Tears of happiness and emotion were shed. Into every inch of the monument had gone Samoa's love and affection—in it is crystallized all the appreciation and estimation of which this whole-souled island race is capable of for their *Makei* and *Kanona*.

More fitting and prophetic was the scriptural analogy raised by Elder McKay in the last discourse delivered by him in Samoa prior to departure from these shores into the great expanse of ocean stretching to the westward, when he quoted and explained as a parting thought Genesis 51:49. *Mizpah* (watchtower) is but one word but expresses a wealth of significance: "The Lord watch between us in our separation!"

# Baby Silita Healed in Samoa

*The following copy of a letter, dated June 3, 1954, from President Howard B. Stone of the Samoan Mission tells of the healing of a native Samoan baby who was stricken ill during the visit of President McKay and Elder Cannon in 1921.*

Dear President McKay:

Last Monday, May 31, was known to all of the Latter-day Saints in Samoa as "McKay Day."

Thirty-three years ago you and Elder Cannon were in Sauniatu, on which occasion you pronounced an apostolic blessing upon the Saints gathered there, and you blessed the land and the village.

This year many of the Saints from our various Church villages met at Sauniatu at 9:30 in the morning. We marched out of the village, past the McKay monument, across the bridge, and were led by the Sauniatu school band back to the place where you stood and gave your blessing to the Saints. After a brief introduction by Uli, the branch president, Laita, the chairman of the supervisory committee, gave a very spiritual invocation, after which the congregation sang *"Fa'afetai Mo Le Perofeta"* ("We Thank Thee, O God, for a Prophet"). Following this song, Folau, a member of the Sauniatu Branch presidency, gave a history of your visit, telling about your traveling from Sauniatu toward the ocean on horseback, then turning the horses around toward Sauniatu and returning to the spot by the side of the road where there now stands a monument painted white with a "1921" printed on it, and which incidentally was adorned with a huge wreath of hibiscus, roses, ferns, and other flowers and vines. He pointed out the *pulu* (rubber tree) where you hung your umbrella during your speech.

There were several people there who were in attendance during your other visit. Sister Sapi Purcell told us all about the blessing which you gave to her sick baby, Silita, who had actually passed away and had turned black. He was restored to life and is now a healthy young man living in New Zealand with his family.

The day was spent in feasting, games, and native dances. Everyone expressed his gratitude for your love, devotion, and great assistance to the Samoan people. All prayers included supplication to our Heavenly Father for your continued health and a deep and sincere desire that you will again be able to return to Samoa, this fall if possible, to dedicate the chapel and school at Sauniatu.

Much more could be related in this letter concerning the impressive events of the day; however because of your very busy daily schedule, I do not feel that I should write a lengthy letter at this time for you to read.

May the Lord bless and sustain you.

Very faithfully your brother,
/signed/ Howard B. Stone

# Return to Sauniatu

*On January 15, 1955, President McKay, in company with Sister McKay, returned to Sauniatu, Samoa, and visited the spot on which the monument had been erected in honor of his visit thirty-four years before. The following is recorded in the day-by-day journal of President McKay's diary to the South Sea Island missions by Elder Franklin J. Murdock.*

Following the King's *kava* ceremonies held in the Pesega Samoan Council House, during which President McKay and his party met all the high chiefs, we took a beautiful drive to Sauniatu to dedicate the new school and other buildings established there. As we neared the valley, which is about a twenty-two-mile drive from Apia, the country takes on a mountainous terrain, resembling the Yellowstone Park area. Tall mountain peaks, heavily wooded, with acres of coconut trees and rushing mountain streams are thrilling to see. This is the most beautiful spot we have as yet seen. This place is very dear to President McKay's heart because of events that transpired thirty-four years ago.

As we crossed the bridge and looked up at the beautiful white monument that the people of Sauniatu erected in memory of President McKay's visit, we could feel the spirit of welcome, progress, and beauty. We received the impression that here is where the "pure in heart" dwell. All the homes are clean, beautifully landscaped, and orderly. Being elevated, it could well be a perfect setting for people who live the gospel.

A fifty-voice choir stood by the monument, and as the Prophet approached they sang "We Thank Thee, O God, for a Prophet." We all wept tears of joy and thanksgiving to be at this spot on this day.

It had rained all week, but this day must be beautiful, *and it was*, with blue skies and warm sunshine!

We all walked slowly to the meeting, and for the next two hours one of the most beautiful services I have ever attended was conducted. President McKay rose to the occasion and brought such a rich spirit of thankfulness and appreciation to the people that they all listened intently to every word. We could have gone on in such a spirit all day, but we had to leave for Apia, where the people were waiting to hold a meeting that evening.

*President Howard B. Stone, president of the Samoan Mission at the time of President McKay's 1955 visit, gives the following report concerning the services held at the monument and at the dedicatory services of the new Sauniatu chapel.*

We paused briefly at the stone erected about one-half mile out of the village of Sauniatu, which bore the date 1921, representing the year that David O. McKay hung his umbrella on the kapoc tree nearby and dismounted from his horse to give the Saints and village a memorable apostolic blessing. This concrete monument was partially surrounded by a hedge, beautifully decorated with an assortment of tropical flowers.

We continued to the Sauniatu River and parked our cars. There were several carloads of Saints, six buses filled with visiting Saints, and a large number of others already waiting for us in the village. As we crossed the bridge, we beheld the beautiful David O. McKay Monument, freshly painted in white, showing a beautiful gold plaque. It was surrounded by flowers and low hedges, spelling out the name Sauniatu. It was indeed a beautiful sight to behold.

As we continued up the incline and walked to the "Welcome Arch," we passed through two lines of Saints all clothed in white. We proceeded to the top of the incline and stood at the end of the village looking toward the chapel. We could see many beautiful red tin-roofed buildings on both sides of the road.

Hedges were trimmed and decorated with hibiscus flowers; lawns were freshly cut; and clusters of tropical blooms were growing profusely and abundantly in well-kept gardens—truly a Garden of Eden! As we stood there, President McKay choked up, and tears came to his eyes as he whispered, "Truly, this is the most beautiful place I have ever seen!"

We walked down to the end of the village to attend dedicatory services of the new Sauniatu church edifice. The Saints followed us, and within a few minutes the new chapel was packed with Saints and investigators. In fact, the building was overflowing and could not begin to accommodate the large crowd of people.

A two-hour meeting was held. Speakers were President Howard B. Stone, President D'Monte Coombs, President Franklin J. Murdock, Sister McKay, and President McKay. At the conclusion of President McKay's soul-stirring and inspirational address, he delivered the dedicatory prayer.

More than six hundred Saints were in attendance. More beautiful songs were sung by the congregation and the Sauniatu District choir. Following this most impressive service, we all returned to Pesega.

# The Story of Ah Ching

*A true faith-promoting story of Ah Ching, a Chinese member of the Church in Samoa, as told by President McKay, June 4. 1921.*

Confucius once said, "All my knowledge is strung on one thread"; and on that "one connecting thread," we learn from his disciple, Tsang Tsu, were hung the principles of self-control and charity to one's neighbor. These are certainly two fundamental elements in character building, without which no man can justly claim true nobility.

I thought I saw the fruits of these two principles exemplified in the life of Ah Ching as I listened to him one day when he and his wife, his son Arthur, and Telese (Mrs. Arthur Ah Ching) acted as hosts to a number of missionaries. That Saturday afternoon and evening, June 4, is numbered among the most pleasant of the many delightful days and nights spent in "dear old" Samoa. Every hour seemed rich in fruition of profitable intercourse and valued friendships, of inspirational experiences, not the least interesting of which was Ah Ching's narration of his early life in these islands. I wish my pen could reproduce his accent and his nervous, animated facial expression as he spoke, in his "pidgin" English mixed with Samoan words, of the trials and reverses and service of those struggling years. But that would be wishing the impossible, so I must be content to write in that old prosaic style which, I fear, is "dry, stale and unprofitable."

Ah Ching is small of stature, about five-feet-five, I should say, and rather lightly built at that. His muscular movements, like his thoughts, indicate a highly nervous temperament. I fancy his temper in his early youth was of the gunpowder type; when touched off, it would go with a flash; and yet, today I believe he can endure imposition and ignominy, if necessary, as patiently as any of his brethren.

If you were to meet him on the street or could see him move unobtrusively into a rear or side seat of church, you would think him, if you gave him even a passing thought, one of the most humble of Chinamen—I'm not sure that your opinion would change, either, if you chanced to see him in his modest three-roomed house in the rear of his little store in Apia. And yet, if you were to offer him a cashier's check of $50,000 for his property interests, he would undoubtedly smile at you, shake his head, and turn to his busy, unassuming life with a view to adding a few more pounds sterling to his comfortable fortune.

This prosperous little businessman "no can lead" (read), he "no can lite" (write); but he can "speakee China, and speakee Samoa." He keeps no books and has never kept an account in his business transactions; but he has never purchased an article in his life without paying spot cash for it. He has never "owed a man a penny." He quickly remarked, "If any man no payee me, please himself, me no care."

Now undoubtedly, in this old workaday, business world, which in many of its aspects seems a long way from that anticipated time when every man will esteem his neighbor as himself, and there shall be no rogues to defraud and to steal, an X-ray examination into Ah Ching's business might reveal the fact that not a few men have "pleased themselves" not to "payee" all they owe him. At any rate there was one who deliberately planned to defraud him and whose dastardly treachery was the means of testing Ah Ching in life's crucible. Had his character not possessed more pure gold than dross, he would perhaps even now be deprived of life or be still wearing the stripes of a condemned felon.

Ah Ching was a young man in his teens when he left Puchow, Fukien Province, China, and enlisted as one of the crew of a small vessel sailing for the South Seas. True to his thrifty nature, acquired by heredity and necessity, he saved nearly every penny of his fair wage. Thus after ten years' constant service with the ship's company, he had accumulated a thousand pounds sterling or more. A business friend whom he had met during his not infrequent visits to Apia induced him to invest his hard-earned savings in a hotel and store, he to furnish the money, his friend to furnish the brains and business acumen required, and the two to divide the profits upon a proportionate basis acceptable to both. Ah Ching invested his money, only to discover in a year or two that he had been robbed of every penny of his hard-earned savings. In certain transfers of the property, it seems his friend had appropriated everything to himself. Trusting Ah Ching couldn't "leadee," couldn't "litee," so he became an unsuspecting victim to the treachery of one to whom he had entrusted practically his life; for "you take one's life, when you take away the means whereby one lives," and up to that time Ah Ching had had but one object and that was to make money, though he had always made it honestly.

When he realized that he had been robbed of all the savings of his young life, when he sensed the villainy of the dishonest scoundrel whom he had called friend, all the fire in his Chinese nature flashed forth and showed him but one more thing for which to live, and that one thing, revenge. He truly wished that his enemy "had forty thousand lives—one was too poor, too weak, to satisfy his revenge."

"He cheatee me all my money; I killee him," he hissed in his rage. "I sharpee a knife like a lacee (razor)," he narrated, indicating the length of the knife by touching with his right hand the elbow of his left arm, which he stretched full length. His knife sharpened, he cried in his agonized rage:

"Me killee him!

"Something inside me say, 'No killee him'; I stop; and it say again, 'No killee him.'

"Then I know God, he helpee me, so I no killee him. I cly (cry), that is all—just cly."

Who can deny that God did "helpee" him in this great crisis of his life? Whether that help sprang from an unsullied conscience or gave strength in a moment of weakness to a will that once more assumed the mastery of a passion, or whether his spirit responded to the promptings of the infinite—the fact remains that his frenzy was overpowered, his spirit subdued, and he just "clied."

Unfortunately, too many fail to heed the gentle "something inside," and follow the lead of blinded passion—whether mental or physical—to their inevitable end, unhappiness, and unescaped misery.

It was not an easy matter for Ah Ching to cry down to his injured and revengeful spirit; but once he became victor, he felt, though he did not then know, that, "vengeance is mine; and I will repay, saith the Lord." (Rom. 12:19.)

It was a real joy to all who heard him relate his experience to see his face light up as he said, "Me gladee from that day to this."

Truly, the fruits of that Spirit are love, joy, and peace.

"Well, how did the man prosper with his stolen money, Brother Ah Ching?" I asked.

"That house he burnee down," he answered, "man in the stleet—all bowed down—nobody likee him—die poor." This intimation that God had avenged his enemy recalled the lines:

> *I know that each sinful action,*
> *As sure as the sun brings shade,*
> *Is somewhere, sometime punished ahead of him,*
> *Though the hour be long delayed.*

With prospects of success ahead of him, Ah Ching had married a chieftain's daughter. Now they were homeless and penniless, except for the money earned day by day at odd jobs. To add to his difficulty, he had voluntarily proffered support to two of his fellow countrymen, one of whom was sickly and unable to supply the least of his necessities. I do not now recall, if I learned at all, what claim the other man had.

"Were they your relatives?" I inquired, knowing the strong ties of family relationship in the Chinese mind.

"No," was his reply, "no lelation—just Chinamen, that's all—needee help, and I give him—I findee wolk sometimee; my woman she takee in washing. Sometimee me have no lice (rice) for all, but me givee Chinamen lice ale samee."

Sharing his last kernel of rice with a fellowman in need, and that, too, without any recompense or desire for reward—is not that true service? No doubt the gratitude whispered by the sick and dying man fully repaid Ah Ching for his years of gratuitous food and shelter; but there will be further recompense when One who takes note of all such kindnesses will someday say,

*These deeds shall thy memorial be—*
*Fear not, thou didst them unto me.*

It is no wonder that the sound of the gospel struck a responsive chord in this humble man's heart—conscientiousness, self-mastery, service among its principal themes.

His Church record, like his life, is marked not in words but in deeds. You may know his annual income by his tithes and offerings, which are freely and thankfully given as expressions of his gratitude for the manifest goodness of God to him.

His rise from poverty to opulence began about the time that he joined the Church, the turning point being marked in his mind, as undoubtedly it was in reality, by a singular dream that came to him.

"I dleamed one night," he narrated, "that the Lord, he say to me, 'Plenty money in the stleet, why you no pick him up?' Next morning I get up, lookee in the stleet—no money. I could see no money in the stleet. Then I thought, I sellee things in the stleet, and makee money."

With the little savings he and his wife had hoarded, he purchased, by paying cash in full, one case of salmon, one sack of sugar, one gross of matches, five plugs of Samoan tobacco, one hundred pounds of Samoan *kava*, and 900 pounds of flour. When this was sold he purchased more. Thus began his little business, which today includes three separate stores and a bakery, all free from encumbrances and carrying on a thriving trade.

His faithful wife, who shared his struggles in poverty, lived to share only a part of his prosperity. A year or so after her death he married her sister, who evidently is an excellent helpmeet and companion to him, and in whom we thought we could detect the same admirable qualities of womanhood as those elements of manhood which have contributed to the commendable life of her husband. Through her lineage he now holds the title of chief among her people.

Of his sons and daughters, we learned but little. His son Arthur, who is now a partner in the business, was educated in China, where his father supported him seven years. He and his wife, Telese, are also members of the Church and seem to hold the confidence and esteem of the mission authorities and elders who know them. They are certainly as bounteous in their desires to please and to serve others as their father Ah Ching; for after eighteen or more feasted that afternoon with all the delicacies Samoa produces, all the Sauniatu band boys were feted to their appetites' content.

As we sat in his flower-bedecked home in Tulaele, with evidences of thrift and prosperity on every hand, as we thought of the number of men and women whom it is in his power now to bless, as we heard him express his gratitude for what the gospel has brought him and for what it means to him, there passed quickly in my mind, in striking contrast to this scene of success and sweet contentment, a picture of a possible felon's cell with all its associated misery and ignominy.

Conscientiousness, service, thrift, honesty, and obedience to other principles of the gospel have given Ah Ching this comfort, and self-mastery in a moment when he stood blindly at the parting of life's ways kept him from the felon's cell.

With the results of his industry around him, and the fruit of the Spirit in his soul, it was indeed gratifying to hear him acknowledge God's guidance and inspiration in this simple sentence:

"Me knowee God, he helpee me."

# An Experience
# on a Sailing Vessel

*Taken from President David O. McKay's world tour diary, Thursday, June 30, 1921, in the Tongan Mission, Nukualofa, Tonga.*

Awoke at 4:00 A.M., and couldn't sleep again, thinking about conditions here, and the duties of the day. At six o'clock the band came and played, and at 6:30, Brother Coombs, Mataila, and I were in the auto on our way to Haateiko to look at a site for the school. (President Cannon had proceeded ahead to New Zealand.)

When we returned, the Relief Society had spread a repast of which all who were leaving for Haapai and Vavau partook, during speeches of praise and appreciation. The rest of the day was spent in saying farewell to individuals and families who called for parting handshakes.

At 3:30 P.M. Mataila's young son drove us to the wharf in his auto. Here a crowd of the Saints had already assembled to bid us farewell. Fua carried one of my satchels from the auto to the boat, and cried all the while as we walked slowly toward the other friends. It seemed that he just could not say the last goodbye. After I shook hands with all the others, he grasped my hand again and made no effort to keep back his sobbing.

The signal was given for all aboard, but as I stepped on the edge of the boat, Fua still held my hand in a lingering grip. As I withdrew he turned and passed through the crowd crying as if he had parted from his father.

A half dozen or more Nukualofa young men were on the boat as it began to move from the pier. When they came to say goodbye—"*Alofa*"—I became somewhat excited, and said, "Better jump off, the boat is moving."

They didn't seem to understand me and appeared so unconcerned that I concluded they were going with us, and wondered why they were saying goodbye. However, I was mistaken in this, for when we were about a quarter of a mile from shore, one after another, extending a last farewell greeting, plunged from the boat into the sea and started back to the waving crowd on the wharf. As they swam, they would turn every now and again and wave their hands above the water. One took off his *lava lava* and flourished it above his head with one hand while he swam or supported himself with the other.

The quaint island town of Nukualofa in the background, the post office, flagpole, and wharf to the fore, the friends waving hats and handkerchiefs on the pier, these dark-colored fluffy heads bobbing up and down in the water, hands and *lava lavas* indicating their fond farewell—these make up my last mental picture of Tongatabu!

I then turned my attention to the old *Tarawa*, a sailing vessel commonly known as a "catch." Seventy of us, natives and whites, were crowded on the deck, each one crouching, kneeling, or reclining on a space only sufficiently large for a common-sized dog to lie comfortably in. I was fairly at ease from hips up, as I reclined on top of the hatch, but my legs hung over, and my feet rested on gasoline cases.

We had left promptly at four o'clock, but the captain exerted no effort to make speed. In fact, he told me that he would sail slowly because he did not want to reach the reefs near Namulue. I learned also that this was the first time he had taken a boat over this particular route.

He seemed a pleasant sort of fellow, and I thought more highly of him when he gave his berth up to Sister Coombs, who became sick as soon as we put to sea.

With a *gatu* rug under me and my steamer rug over me, which I shared with Brother Coombs and Brother May, I cuddled up in my corner and prepared for an uncomfortable night. As soon as the sun went down, a cold stiff breeze came up, making matters pretty disagreeable. Dozens of people became ill. I rather enjoyed seeing Brother Coombs shoot for the rail, followed by two or three other elders. but I felt sorry for the women.

About eight o'clock, Captain Doughty came over to me and said, "You're not comfortable there, Mr. McKay. I've given up my berth, but the engineer's is just opposite it. Won't you occupy it?"

The young engineer urging me to do so, I accepted, leaving my space and rugs to the others.

I had been down only a short time before I was using the mug when Sister Coombs wasn't. The sea was rough, and the boat rolled and pitched as if it were a shell. I could hear the waters swishing above me and feel the waves strike the sides with blows that made the craft quiver.

At 11:30 the captain came down and examined his chart once again, as he had done frequently during the last two or three hours, and I noticed that his movements were unsteady; but I concluded that the responsiblity of running the boat in the darkness in a tempestuous sea was fatiguing him. When he threw himself on the seat alongside the berth I occupied, I offered him my place, but he refused. Then it was that I fancied I smelled whiskey. The thought that his unsteady movement was due to drink almost chilled my blood. But I couldn't believe any man would run such a risk as to become intoxicated on a wild night with seventy men and women and children packed on the deck like cargo.

I was very sick by this time, and my fears only aggravated my condition. Soon he began to cough, and I recognized it as a whiskey cough.

The boat gave a sudden lurch to starboard, and the skipper was thrown in a heap on the floor. He fell like so much sand. With curses under his breath, he struggled back to the bench and again stretched himself for a sleep. The engineer came down, asked something about the sails, which I could not understand, received a curt reply, with an order to call the captain at two o'clock.

I did not know what was going on above, but the way the boat plunged and rolled, and the waters beat above us, the sea seemed to be mad. Another sudden lurch, and again off rolled the skipper. This time he lay where he fell. Then I saw for the first time that he was holding a quart bottle of whiskey.

I've been in a number of serious predicaments; I've faced a few dangers and have met with serious accidents, but I've never experienced such forebodings in my life as came over me as I lay there trying to decide what could be done. There was a combination of evils that would be hard to duplicate. Seasickness—midnight—an ocean vessel containing seventy people—a mad sea—reefs ahead— and the captain drunk!

I decided at once that he would drink no more from that bottle, so I reached down and slid it, unseen or unfelt by him, under my pillow.

Now we must trust to the young engineer to hold that wheel and manage the vessel as ordered until 2:30. Perhaps by that time the captain's snooze would sober him a bit. But he soon awoke, felt around for his bottle, got up, looked about him, opened a cupboard door, felt among some maps, then lit a cigarette and went up on deck.

I rid my stomach of accumulated bile and threw myself again in my bunk. Just as I began to doze, the captain came down again and began to fumble among some packages in the opposite corner of the cabin. He has another whiskey bottle, I thought. I spoke to him, and he jerked his arm back, picked up a towel, and began to wipe his face. Then I knew that he surmised that I had his bottle and was sensible enough to know why. I also knew that he wouldn't drink while I watched him.

And that is what I did all night. Not a wink of sleep from 11:30 P.M. until 6 A.M. Oh, what a night! Talk about the perils of the sea!

At 3 A.M. the engineer came down and said, "Three o'clock, sir, we've tacked."

That meant that they had turned the boat to face the wind, had arranged the sails to keep her there, tied the steering wheel, and let her drift. In changing the sails and turning, the boat was thrown into a trough of the sea and completely covered by a mountainous wave, which deluged everyone on deck except the native and Sister Coombs' nine-month-old baby whom she was holding.

Lui Wolfgramme, a native weighing 215 pounds, was lifted up entirely from the deck, and in the darkness he thought he had been washed overboard, wrapped in his *tapu* cloth. The lifeboat was lifted up and fell again on one of the native women's legs, nearly breaking them. Brother Clark, of Eden, was thrown over the rail. He saved himself from going overboard by catching hold of a rope, and sixty-seven other lives in equal peril because the captain was not at his post!

Two of the elders—Sorenson and Phillips—drenched and cold and so sick they could not hold up their heads, came down the steps, or rather fell down, and lay on the floor to keep warm. Getting no more opportunity to drink, the skipper was ready to take charge of the boat about daylight, and we hoisted sails and continued once more on our journey to Haapai, where we arrived without mishap at six o'clock that evening (Friday, July 1st), a weak, bedraggled, but grateful crowd—thankful to the Lord for our lives and power to walk once again on land.

We were greeted at the wharf by a group of warmhearted, expectant friends, who, with flashlights and lanterns, conducted us to the conference house. Here we changed our clothes, the men shaved, we ate a bite (the first in twenty-four hours or more), and at nine o'clock held meeting with 116 people who assembled at that hour for worship.

After administering to two adults and blessing a baby, I said "Good night," and threw my weary body and tired brain, but buoyant, thankful spirit, upon one of the cleanest, most neatly prepared beds of the trip!

*Saturday, July 2, 1921*

The captain had promised to leave at seven this morning, so we might arrive at Vavau this evening. Consequently, we were astir early in preparation for sailing. While at breakfast we received word that the boat could not sail until ten o'clock.

The tide ebbed, and we did not leave Haapai until 1:15 P.M. It should be said, however, to the captain's credit that he would have sailed earlier if the gasoline launch, on which he depended to tow the *Tarawa* to deep water, had not lost its rudder. Just before we started, he said to me, "If it weren't for the fact that it would interfere with your plans, I would not start at this hour of the day. It will be dark before we can pick up the islands."

"It's safe to enter Vavau harbor after dark, is it not, captain?" said I.

"Oh, yes, if we can sight the islands."

"Well, let's go," I suggested.

With "flying jib," "jib sail," "fore stay sail," "main sail," and "spanker" all spread to the wind, and the engine running as well, we sped over the waves in good time. For two hours or more we made good headway.

It was an interesting experience to see how skillfully Captain Doughty could strike the waves, ride their crest, then dive into the trough without having the waves dash over the boat. The sea was rough, and every few moments a wave would come rolling high above, threatening to submerge us, but we found ourselves always on top.

Passengers began to get sick about sundown, when the wind became stronger and the sea rougher.

A woman, her sixteen-year-old daughter, and her little three-year-old boy occupied a space opposite mine on the hatch. I suggested that she go down and occupy the berth I had the night before, but she wanted to "stay above to see what was going on."

In a few minutes I saw that pale green color around her mouth, and I knew she would soon be as sick as her daughter who already spent all her time at the rail. Before midnight they would both, perhaps all three, be unable to move.

"Lady," I suggested, "your staying on deck will make no difference to the sailing of the boat; the captain will run it just the same. You had better go below while the going is good."

"Oh yes, thank you, I believe I will. I must go somewhere!"

She and her boy were very ill all night, and so was the young girl who remained on deck. Fortunately, I was all right, and was comforted, as I watched the captain, to discern that he was not drinking beer after he left Haapai, and I knew he had no whiskey.

Darkness came on, the wind became fierce, and the waves madder. I felt that the captain was sailing too far west and so expressed myself to Brother Robinson, but it seemed presumptuous for me to suggest it. About ten o'clock, a sailor was up in the rigging peering out into the darkness to spy an island, but none could be seen.

There was nothing to do but "tack" for the night, which we

did. I gave my robe to a native girl who lay on the deck below with one of Brother Coombs' little children. Though I was not sick, I could not sleep, so I lay all night watching the Southern Cross and other heavenly galaxies as they moved in their "appointed order and unvarying course."

At four o'clock, the crescent moon came up, and about that hour I felt the young English girl shivering. As I tried to tuck the robe around her shoulders, she said, "Thank you, it's no use, for my feet are wet, my clothes are wet, my hair is wet. You've done all you can to make me comfortable, I'm sure, unless you throw me overboard; and that's the sensible thing to do. Death has lost all terrors for me!"

In the dim light of the moon and morning star, the captain ordered sails adjusted, turned the ship again, and once more started toward Vavau; but I noticed he sailed almost in an easterly direction—he had drifted west, as I had surmised.

Just as the sun arose, a wave dashed over the deck, deluging and drenching us all to the skin. The two little boys, crying, wet, and cold, were carried down to the parents, and the two native girls, Takou and Seni, sat up and used my robe, which is almost waterproof as well as cold proof. The young girl huddled close to my left, so cold and sick that she could scarcely hold up her head.

It was three P.M. before we were safely landed at Vavau.

*Later, when President McKay was making a report of this world tour to members of the Church assembled in general conference, April 6, 1922, he referred to the above experience and said, "I knew of His protecting care in the Tongan Islands; for when the vessel was submerged by a mountainous wave, we felt peace and security."*

*M. Vernon Coombs, who was president of the Tongan Mission, was also on board this sailing vessel. A report by him of this experience was published in the March 1922 issue of* The Improvement Era, *excerpts from which follow:*

The sails were all set, and we were looking forward to an interesting voyage, for this was the first time that some of our elders, with Brother McKay and Sister Coombs, had experienced a voyage at sea in a sailing vessel. At first we had a pleasant wind, and all were in the best spirits. Everything went along splendidly until dusk. We had cleared the dangers as well as the protection afforded by the outer reefs and were out on the open sea. Without warning, a heavy wind came up which made the boat behave in such a fashion that we elders, and many of the natives, were suddenly reminded that the rail was a pretty good friend upon which to lean in case of an emergency. Even Brother McKay, experienced sailor that he now is, was glad to avail himself of the mate's unoccupied berth. The tiny craft rocked, leapt, careened and rolled from side to side in a manner that beggars all description, while wave after wave broke on the deck causing the cans of kerosene to bang and float about creating a horrid din. The wind howled in the rigging like a maniac straining at the bands with which he was bound. At irregular intervals a flash of lightning would make the scene more vivid. We were drenched time and time again by the heavy seas, which came thundering over the rails, and all the time we were clinging on for dear life, for to be washed overboard would have been the last of us. The captain was drinking heavily and but for the heroic vigil kept by Elder McKay, he would have completely incapacitated himself. The helm was lashed down and the boat was left with no one to guide her and to drift as best she might for the night. There was more than one prayer for safety offered during the course of that night. My consolation and assurance lay in the promise of President Penrose that I should go in safety on both land and sea.

During the night the only lifeboat was washed loose and hit with a sickening thud on the leg of a poor old sister who as a result has lain in the hospital for eight weeks. The vessel went on her very side, and the luggage and boxes and sacks of flour came down in an avalanche on those poor women and children in the hold, but fortunately no one was hurt. Our three children were in there. Two of the elders were all but washed overboard, and but for their becoming entangled in the rigging would not have been with us at the end of that voyage.

As the wind continued to increase in force, the half-drunken captain came on deck to see if he could not do something to mitigate our danger from being swamped. All sails were taken in but the main sail, and this was made as small as possible by reefing, for the rudder had split, and too much strain might render it completely useless. The wind was so strong that the captain was afraid to change the course of the boat by tacking lest when the sail was changed to the opposite side, the vessel be swamped or the mast snapped off by the force of the wind. One of the good Saints, Lui Wolfgramme, then took the helm and stayed with it all day and piloted us through the intricate passages of the Haapai reef. That morning we saw in the distance a small boat, the *Malolo,* with all sails down, drifting helplessly. We learned afterward that her crew had given up hope and after taking down the sails had thrown out two anchors before going below the deck in the desperate hope that one or both of them might catch on to something and thus save the little raft from drifting onto the treacherous reef. It was twenty-eight hours of such experiences.

Truly President Penrose must have been prompted by the Spirit of God when he pronounced blessings upon Sister Coombs and me. Then, too, Elder McKay was aboard that vessel as a special envoy of The Church of Jesus Christ of Latter-day Saints, to visit the nations of the world in the interests of the Church. Verily, yes, the Lord will protect his faithful servants in the performance of their duties!

# In the Holy Land

*Taken from President McKay's world tour diary,* October 31, 1921.

When we awoke this morning, the sun was shining, and we were still speeding toward Jerusalem. The country through which we were traveling was sandy and bare. Trains of heavily laden camels and donkeys with their plodding drivers, sticks in hands, were seen in the distance continually.

Although the country is barren and desert-like, it needs only a little water to make it produce fruitfully. This was evidenced by the groves of orange and olive trees that we saw near one of the stations.

As we neared Bitter, we caught our first glimpse of the terraced hillsides, their green garden truck and grape vines standing out in striking contrast to the rocky, barren limestone hills through which we had been traveling.

At Bitter, too, I first heard the name "Bethlehem" spoken in Palestine. It was by a poor but beautiful Arabian girl, offering grapes for sale. When asked if these were grown in the village, she replied, "No, these came from Bethlehem," indicating with a slight nod of her head that Bethlehem was just over the hill to the south.

As we left this town, we caught glimpses of trenches on the hillside, grim but forceful reminders of the recent war [World War I] that decided the fate, not only of Palestine but also to a degree of the whole world.

The first view I had of Jerusalem was from the car window, at about 12:15 P.M. A walled city of white, flat-roofed houses, with the lofty Russian tower standing on the Mount of Olives nearby—this was my first mental picture of this, the most historic place in the world.

Leaving our baggage in charge of a hotel runner, we stepped into a cab and were driven to the Allenby Hotel, just outside the walls near the Jaffa Gate on the southwest side of the city.

A bath, change of clothes, and lunch made us forget the hot, dusty ride, but made us even more eager for the post office to open so that we could get anticipated mail from home. At 3:00 P.M. we were standing in front of the "Post Restante" window and were not disappointed, thanks to the thoughtfulness and sweetness of my sweetheart and the good foresight of our missionary son, David L.— newsy, loving letters from each, with another enclosed in Ray's, also a copy of the letter President Grant sent me in Australia.

Toward evening we walked through the Jaffa Gate and into old Jerusalem. We did not then notice the small iron door in the large gate, which was called the "eye of the needle." (See Matt. 19:20.) Neither did we know that the Tower of David was on our right. Having decided to start sightseeing in the morning with a competent guide, we were simply reconnoitering. Keeping straight ahead, we entered David Street and found ourselves walking down stone steps. Some distance down, we turned to the right into another narrow street crowded with all kinds of people and donkeys. Many of the people showed by their features and dress that they are foreign Jews.

After a half hour's stroll, we returned to the hotel and wrote notes. Our rooms are small and barely furnished, but fairly comfortable. Rate: 120 piastres ($4.20) per day including meals.

*Tuesday, November 1, 1921*

When we secured our dragoman last night for two days' sightseeing, he said we would go by auto to Bethlehem first this morning; but when we met him at 8:00 A.M. he suggested that we order a lunch prepared and make the trip today to Jericho and the Dead Sea.

Accordingly, within a very short time we were in a Ford rattling toward the valley of the Jordan. At the post office we turned to the right passing the following gates in the order named: (1) the New Gate, (2) Damascus Gate, Camel's Entrance, (3) Herod's Gate, (4) St. Stephen's Gate, (5) Beautiful Gate.

Just before we descended into the Valley of Jehosophat, we passed on our right the spot on which Stephen, the first Christian martyr, was stoned to death while Saul, then a young man and a persecutor of the hated sect of Nazarenes, held the cloaks of some of the murderers.

We crossed the Brook Kedron and passed the Garden of Gethsemane on our left, concluding to enter it upon our return. With the same thought in mind, we also passed Bethany, the home of Mary, Martha, and Lazarus.

I was impressed with the Apostles' Fountain, not because of what our guide told us, for he was wrong, but because, undoubtedly, Jesus and his disciples often stopped at this well or spring to refresh themselves.

Our dragoman told us that was the spot where the Savior told his disciples that "Lazarus sleeps: but I go to waken him." (See John 11:11.) According to John, that circumstance or conversation took place while they were still in Perea.

The rough, mountainous country through which we were passing must have furnished an excellent rendezvous for robbers in olden days; and its rugged, barren appearance helped us to believe that the good Samaritan Inn, or wayside *Khan* that was built along this road, the ruins of which may still be seen a short distance from the inn still in service, was the one Jesus had in mind when he gave the parable of the good Samaritan. (Luke 10.) Not far from this place is the scene where the prophet Elijah was fed by the ravens. (1 Kings 17.)

We wondered when we saw some very large quail or small pheasants, and observed how tame they are, if the Old Testament "ravens" were not these birds. Anyhow, we could well believe the account in Exodus wherein it states that the Israelites were furnished quail in such abundance that they could catch them with little or no trouble.

I was not disappointed in the Jordan Valley, although it is dry and barren of all vegetation except a shrub that resembles our greasewood and rabbitbrush.

The Dead Sea is 1,293 feet below the level of the sea and 3,786 feet lower than Jerusalem. Its shoreline is the lowest part of the earth's surface not covered with water.

It is a beautiful body of water, and this day it was exceptionally so because the surface was sufficiently stirred to make the waves high and boisterous as they splashed against the pebbly shore. We tried to secure a boat to row on it, but a man at a little station on the northern shore said it was too rough. We hired a native to swim out and secure two bottles of the clean water as specimens. It contains twenty-five percent mineral salt.

Across the sea to the east and running north and south are the mountains of Moab. There stands Mt. Nebo from which Moses viewed the Promised Land. (Deut. 34.) It was near Mt. Nebo that Elijah was taken up to heaven. (2 Kings 2.)

Leaving the Dead Sea, we drove north through high, dense weeds or shrubs to the traditional place on the Jordan River where the children of Israel crossed into the Promised Land. Perhaps in that same vicinity the Savior of the world was baptized "to fulfil all righteousness."

Between the Jordan and Jericho, we were shown the place where, at Gilgal, Joshua erected the pillar of twelve stones. (Josh. 4.) As we stood near the tree which marks the spot, our guide pointed out the site of the ancient Sodom from which Lot and his family fled (Gen. 19), and also the place where Lot's wife was turned into a pillar of salt.

Jericho today is a fertile spot standing near the site of the ancient city. Soudan Bedouins are the principal inhabitants of the small, dirty town. Orange and banana trees flourish here. At this place we were shown the beautiful pool known as "Elisha's Fountain." (2 Kings 2, 19-22.) They are just below the excavated ruins of the old Jericho, down the walls of which Rahab assisted Joshua's spies to escape. (Josh. 19.) A portion of the walls of her house may still be seen. Jericho was the home of Zacchaeus and of the blind Bartimaeus.

The lofty mountain in the southwest is known as Mt. Temptation. Here is the supposed scene of the Savior's fasting and temptation.

Upon our return in the afternoon, we visited the tomb of Lazarus at Bethany and the ruins of the two rooms in which Mary and Martha so often entertained their Lord. Mohammedans now own the place, and a dirty, dingy place it is, too, but I was all the while picturing in my mind the happy scenes that occurred here about 2,000 years ago, so I did not mind the debris and filth. I recognized no Marys nor Marthas in any of the women we passed in this place much visited by the Master.

We visited the Garden of Gethsemane, now the property of Franciscan Fathers. As at every other sacred spot in Jerusalem there are too many modern things around here to realize at first that this is the garden to which Jesus and his disciples repaired so frequently for prayer; but the rock—thank heaven they can't change that—on which the three disciples sat and "watched" is sufficiently natural to make one partly picture the scene as it was on the fatal night when Judas betrayed his Lord.

Although it was nearly 3:30 o'clock, we concluded that we still had time to drive to Bethlehem, six miles south of Jerusalem. Before starting, however, we visited the Church of the Virgin, which marks the spot where the mother of the Savior was buried. An automobile was waiting for us near the place where Stephen was martyred, so before taking my seat, I stood a moment on what might have been the very spot from which, just before he died, he saw the heavens open.

We passed the hotel on our way to Bethlehem, drove by the

Jaffa Gate, and entered the Valley of Hinnom, a deep ravine that bounds Jerusalem on the south. This was the ancient boundary between Judah and Benjamin. On the south side of this is the Hill of Evil Counsel where the Jews counseled how to put Jesus to death and where Solomon had built an altar to Moloch.

The Valley of Gehenna (or hell), where the fires burning the refuse of the city were never quenched, was on our left. On the slope of this hill to the left of the present road crossing the valley are several cemeteries, one of which is known as Aceldama, or Field of Blood, said to be the Potters' Field which was purchased with the thirty pieces of silver for which Judas betrayed his Lord. (Matt. 27.) A short distance past the station, we drove through the Valley of Rephaim or Valley of Giants, where David twice defeated the Philistines. (2 Samuel 5.)

About halfway between Jerusalem and Bethlehem is the Well of the Magi, by the side of which Mary sat on her way to Bethlehem. A little farther on is Rachel's Tomb, where Jacob "set up a pillar upon her grave." (Genesis 35 and 1 Samuel 10:2.)

The cold west wind blowing this afternoon and evening made us realize more keenly what hardships Mary would have endured had she entered Bethlehem as late as we were on the evening of December 24. Fortunately for her, she and Joseph entered the town in the month of April.

Off to our left were the Well of David and the field where the "shepherds were watching their flocks by night."

Bethlehem is a city of about 3,000, nearly all of whom profess to be Christians. Over the *Khan*, or inn where Christ was born, stands the church built by Constantine, in which Greek Catholics, Roman Catholics, and Armenians respectively have chapels. The silver and the gold decorations and trappings that surround the sacred spot where the child Jesus was born seemed to me to be desecrations. And when our guide pointed out the lines of demarkation between the Greeks and the Latins and the Armenians and told us how they fought each other if one happened to trespass upon his neighbor, I was disgusted.

Twenty-five years ago the Armenian Christians, who have just a small corner for their altar, happened to move their carpet off their assigned place while they swept the floor. The consequence was that in the struggle that followed, so our guide reported, three of them were killed. Roman Catholics dare not cross the Greek Catholic part. Pictures hang on the wall, undusted and so begrimed that they cannot be recognized for what they are, but no one dares touch them because the other sects would be so aroused in jealousy. And all this in the very precinct of the spot where was born he whose birth was heralded by a heavenly host singing, "Glory to God in the highest, and on earth *peace,* good will toward men." (Luke 2:14.)

The spirit of contention, of bigotry, and of jealousy has banished the Spirit of the Christ from the place of his nativity! After spending an hour or so in Bethlehem, we returned to Jerusalem.

*Wednesday, November 2, 1921*

When we parted from our guide last night, it was with the understanding that we should go to the Mount of Olives this morning; but we were surprised to learn first thing that the program was changed.

"Don't ask me why I change," said Michael, who seemed somewhat nervous, "just you trust me. I will tell you when we enter the city."

Mr. Spiva and party were also disappointed in not finding their car ready to take them to the Dead Sea. We later learned that every driver was instructed not to run his auto, and that every Mohammedan and every Jewish business house and nearly every Christian place of business was closed for the day.

Said Michael, "This is a day of mourning. Today the Mohammedans and the Christians throughout Palestine unite in protesting against Lord Balfour's declaration that Palestine shall be set apart as a gathering place for the Jews."

This was a revelation to me. At first I was inclined to treat the matter lightly, not crediting our man with a thorough understanding of the matter; but the more we questioned him and the more clearly we discerned his bitter antipathy toward the Jews, the more convinced I became that we were going to witness this day a most significant demonstration.

Not a shop was open! Not a donkey or a camel did we see! Men and women were gathering in groups, and we soon began to feel the spirit of tension in the city.

Michael was vehement—under his breath—in his protestations that the Jews shall never rule Palestine.

Said I, "Michael, standing here on the street of David, this 2nd of November, 1921, I want to tell you something to remember. No matter how much the Mohammedans and the Greek Christians oppose the Jews' coming back to Palestine, the Jews are coming and will possess this land."

"Never," he cried with emphasis and bitterness. "The streets will flow with blood first!"

"The streets may and undoubtedly will flow with blood," I answered, "but that will not prevent the Jews possessing their land. Don't you believe your Bible?"

"I know the Bible says Jerusalem will be rebuilt," was his admission, "but the time hasn't come yet."

"Yes, the time has come."

We had now reached Mt. Moriah and were standing on the site of the outer court of Solomon's temple. The altar of sacrifice was supposed to be on the spot where Abraham was ready to offer Isaac. Suddenly our ears caught the sounds of mingled voices crying something in unison. I started toward the street from which the noise came, and Brother Cannon followed.

"Don't go there! Stop! Come back!" cried Michael. "There will be trouble."

If there was going to be trouble, we wanted to see it, so we did not heed our guide. Modern Jerusalem became more interesting to us than Jerusalem of old. However, it proved to be only a group of college students and a crowd of youngsters yelling, "Allah is our prophet."

Rejoining our guide, who repeated every once in a while, "This is bad. There will be fighting. Some people will be killed," we left the Mosque of Omar, which stands on the old temple site, and made our way to the Church of the Holy Sepulchre. Here gold in great profusion, diamonds, and other precious stones adorn the sacred spot and pictures of Christ and Mary, to the value of millions of dollars. Here, too, the contending sects, in their fanatic zeal to honor their Lord, disgrace themselves and his cause by their jealousy and hatred of one another. We came out from this church sensing the significance of the following expressions by Count Eberhardt of Wurttemberg: "There are three acts in a man's life which no one ought either to advise another to do or not to do. The first is to contract matrimony, the second is to go to the wars, the third is to visit the Holy Sepulchre. I say that these three acts are good in themselves, but they may easily turn out ill; and when this is so, he who gave the advice comes to be blamed as if he were the cause of its turning out ill."

But the climax of the adornment of wealth and costly jewels as a manifestation of adoration is reached in the Church of Calvary. "The King of the Jews," Pilate's inscription over Jesus, is written in twelve large letters, each studded with diamonds! The keys to the Holy Sepulchre are kept by a Moslem because the Christian sects will not trust one of their number with them.

The pool of Bethesda where Christ healed the impotent man (John 5) is a very interesting spot, though somewhat difficult of access. It is many feet below the present surface, but old masonry still reveals the old corridors which in all probability stood when the Savior and his disciples visited the place.

In the Church of the Covenant of the Sisters of Zion, we saw what undoubtedly is the original Roman pavement in the official residence of the Roman governor, and also the remains of the arch through which Christ would pass "when he left the Praetorium bearing the cross on his way to Calvary." I enjoyed my visit to this place and seemed to feel the sanctity which should be associated with these sacred spots more than I have in any of the other churches. It is to be regretted that each spot has not been preserved in its naturalness and simplicity, without being covered up with cold prison-like churches in which worshipers show hatred for each other instead of love.

By this time, 11:30 A.M., there was a good deal of Moslem rowdyism manifest in the narrow streets of the city, and our guide was so worried that his mind was more on what was going to happen than on what happened over 1900 years ago. And so was ours in a very few minutes. As we walked up David Street, we met hundreds of Mohammedans going toward the Mosque of Omar to pray. Suddenly behind them we heard imprecating yells, and mingling with them, cries for help. Hurrying forward, we saw two Jewish women, some children, and one or two men trying to escape from a mob with sticks and stones in their hands, pursuing them like hyenas after prey. I saw one fellow hurl a stone and strike a fugitive man in the back. The women's faces were blanched with fear.

As the Jews fled past us, I raised my cane and cried to the pursuers to stop as they rushed by. Jumping in front of a youngster with a large stone in his hand which he was about to throw, I said, "What are you doing? Put down that stone!"

But he only defied me and tried to pass. Fortunately, policemen had come in behind us and had met the mob, whose impetus was by this time broken, and they were being driven back; but they moved defiantly until an officer came with a whip of two lashes, which he used to good advantage. I have never seen blows given to men and boys that seemed to have been so merited!

A little farther on, we found the entrance to the street leading to what our guide said was the Jewish quarter, well guarded by about a dozen soldiers. Michael turned to the right, but we stopped, desiring to go into this part of the city to see what was going on.

"Come this way," said Michael nervously.

"Let's go up this street," I suggested.

"No, you must not go there; it's not safe!"

"Oh, it is safe enough."

"If you go there, you go alone."

"All right, Michael, here's where you and we part company," I said. "We'll meet you at two o'clock."

With a surprised look our guide turned away and walked rapidly out of the district.

The feeling in the street in which we now found ourselves was truly ominous. Recognizing us as Americans, the soldiers had permitted us to pass; but the huddling groups of foreign Jews seemed to eye us with suspicion. They were frightened but were consulting together and wondering what was going to happen. We tried in vain once or twice to talk to them, but none could understand English. Finally we approached a crowd in which a young man understood us and whom we could understand. In reply to our question as to what the trouble was all about, he said, "The Mohammedans and Christians are opposed to the Zionist movement, and they make this demonstration as a protest against Lord Balfour's declaration that Palestine should be given as a place for the Jews."

We had asked and received answers to only a few questions, when the men whom we could see assembled in an arched hallway ejaculated in what seemed to me to be protesting tones.

"Are they objecting to your talking to us?"

"Yes."

"Well, tell them we're Americans and favor the Jews coming back to Jerusalem. We're Christians."

"Then why do you wear that?" he surprised me by asking, and pointed to my stickpin—the star and crescent.

"That's a present from my wife and has no Moslem significance."

They grouped around me, inspected it closely, and decided it had as much Jewish significance as Moslem, so we seemed to have won favor rather than to have lost it.

I shall never forget that scene in that Jewish street of Jerusalem—frightened women and children on balconies or peering out of windows, men moving about in groups expecting something, or consulting in lowered tones in ominous groups. I seemed to see, not many years hence, those doorways and stone steps covered with blood in the great struggle that is impending, of which the spirit of this day is but the rumbling as of a pent-up volcano. I was glad to see the British "Tommies" around with helmets on their heads and bayonets fixed, and to see the armed motor cars pass through the streets. They had a subduing influence upon the rising spirit of what soon could be a frenzied mob.

When after lunch we met Michael, I said, "How do you do, Michael. You see we are still alive."

"Don't you think I was mistaken," he said gloomily. "As soon as you left that street one man was killed and several others wounded."

"How?"

"By a bomb."

And he told us the truth. A bomb had been thrown into the crowd, killing one man outright, mortally wounding two others, and severely injuring several men.

Later in the day, near the Damascus Gate, three Jews were killed—clubbed and stoned to death in reparation and vengeance. Wild rumors were afloat, and the tension was high, so it was difficult to obtain the real facts of the situation. Official orders were cried throughout the city that no one would be permitted on the streets after 5 o'clock P.M. And that order was implicitly carried out. At six o'clock the streets of Jerusalem were as deserted as a cemetery. Only the soldiers on guard and an occasional warning shot indicated the presence of the ominous spirit of the inhabitants of the Holy Land.

As I sat in my room thinking over the events of the day, only a hint of which I have here given, I was overwhelmed with the thought that we had witnessed on this 2nd of November the manifestation of a smouldering spirit of hatred which will some day in the near future cause much bloodshed.

I realized, too, the necessity of the presence of the British Government as the Protectorate of Palestine, and associated with all the events that have taken place since Lord Balfour's declaration, the prophecy in the Book of Mormon that the Gentiles shall be the means of restoring Israel to the Promised Land.

*Thursday, November 3, 1921*

At 3:30 P.M., Brother Cannon and I walked down David Street, out of the Gate of St. Stephen, across the Brook Kedron, and ascended the Mount of Olives. Here in a secluded spot under a fig tree, nearly opposite the Gate Beautiful, we knelt down and offered up our thanksgiving and praise to our Heavenly Father.

We prayed—

1. That the seed sown during our visits to the various missions on this tour would be blessed and multiplied manyfold.

2. That the Lord would accept our gratitude for the privilege of visiting the Holy Land at this time when the prophecies concerning it are about to be fulfilled—that we are witnesses to the beginning of the great movement that will eventually restore Palestine to the Jews.

3. That the form of worship, the outward semblance of devotion without the true Spirit of the Redeemer, which we have seen manifested at nearly every spot made sacred by the footsteps, teachings, and prayers of the Redeemer, might be replaced by more appropriate memorials and the places themselves surrounded by keepers who are imbued with the spirit of tolerance and love and true Christian service.

4. That the spirit of opposition and hatred which we witnessed yesterday by Moslems and so-called Christians in opposition to the return of the Jews to this land may be overcome. By the power of the priesthood this antagonistic bitterness was rebuked that it should not prevail.

5. That the members of the church of Christ might more earnestly manifest in their daily lives the genuine fruits of the true gospel of the Redeemer, and thus convert the world, who, seeing their good deeds, will be led to glorify their Father in heaven.

6. That the Church and our loved ones may receive special protection and guidance.

7. That we may be led by inspiration on our trip to the Armenian Mission.

Upon returning to the hotel, I felt strongly impressed not to go by automobile tomorrow but by train. The order tonight is that all business is to be suspended and all streets must be cleared by 6:00 P.M.

# A Remarkable
# Meeting in Armenia

*A sacred experience in the Turkish Mission in 1921, written for the* Deseret News, *November 26, 1932.*

On December 2, 1920, the late President Hugh J. Cannon and I were set apart for a special mission, to visit a number of the Latter-day Saint missions in distant parts of the world.

Among these was the Turkish Mission, of which Armenian Saints composed the principal part. It was then in a disorganized state, and the members of the Church who had not been killed during the Great World War or massacred by the Turks were so scattered that it was difficult even to know where they were situated.

December 4, we started on our mission.

In March 1921, we learned that on a special fast day, contributions in the amount of several thousand dollars had been made for relief of the destitute in Europe and the suffering Armenians in Asia. We learned, too, that the First Presidency contemplated sending a special messenger to Syria to render personal aid to our Armenian Saints.

Our mission carried us to the Antipodes, and to a number of the South Sea Isles; so the year 1921 was nearing its close before we found ourselves sailing toward Port Said en route to Syria.

During the months intervening, we had received no word concerning conditions in Armenia. We did not know whether anyone had been sent with relief funds. We knew only that it was our duty to visit that mission and report to the First Presidency of the Church.

Inquiry by cable of the president of the European Mission brought us the information that Elder J. Wilford Booth was on his way to Aleppo. This was good news. The next thing was to locate him. We communicated with the United States Consul at Aleppo, and on November 3, 1921, at Jerusalem received the following telegram:

"Aleppo, November 2, 1921: Informed Booth en route Aleppo. Do not know whereabouts — Jackson."

My diary of that same date reads:

"We have no idea where he is, but shall leave Jerusalem for Haifa, en route to Aleppo, to-morrow morning. Have concluded to go by auto through Samaria, visiting Bible scenes."

At 3:30 P.M. of the same day, we ascended the Mount of Olives, and, choosing a secluded spot near where Jesus is supposed to have stood when he cried: "O Jerusalem, Jerusalem," etc. (Matt. 23:37), we knelt in humble supplication and thanksgiving to God. The substance of our prayer I need not give here, except that we prayed that we should be led by inspiration on our trip to the Armenian Mission.

Upon returning to the hotel, I felt strongly impressed that we should go by train and not by auto to Haifa. When I said as much to President Cannon, he replied, "If you feel that way, we had better take the train."

Our greatest desire as we neared this mission was to meet Elder Booth. Indeed, it seemed that our trip to Syria would be useless unless we should meet him. We were strangers. We knew no one. The branches of the Church in Syria were disorganized. True, we had some names and addresses; but we could not read them, since they were written in the Turkish language. Later, we learned that these addresses, even if we could have found them, were useless. The warning given us not to go to Aintab by a British government official as well as by the United States Consul at Cairo only tended to increase our realization of the need of meeting Brother Booth or some other person who could speak the Turkish language of the country and who knew where we might find our scattered people. We carried in our pockets a letter from President Heber J. Grant received at Jerusalem, in which he, too, expressed the hope that Brother Booth and we might meet.

Carrying out our impression not to go by auto through Samaria, we accordingly left Jerusalem by train at 6:00 A.M., November 4th. We knew that we should be compelled to remain one night at Haifa before continuing our journey to Aleppo. Past experiences, one or two of which had been very annoying, had taught us the advisability of knowing the names of respectable hotels in each strange city we approached. This we usually obtained by inquiry at the town we were just leaving.

Shortly after leaving Jerusalem and before we approached a little town called Bitter, I said to President Cannon, "Did you ask for the name of a hotel at Haifa?"

"No," he replied, "I didn't. Did you?"

Now it was nothing unusual for me to forget a thing like that, but it was for Brother Cannon. Indeed, I do not recall another single important detail on the entire trip which he forgot or overlooked.

We both felt reassured and at our ease when he said, "The Allenby Hotel runner is on this train: I will ask him when we get to Ludd."

But, strange to say, at Ludd we changed trains and were several miles away from there before we realized that neither of us had remembered to speak to the hotel man about a hotel at Haifa.

I have gone into detail about this seemingly insignificant matter because it has direct bearing upon what follows.

Arriving at Haifa, I said to Brother Cannon, "You take care of the luggage here, and I will try to make inquiry regarding a suitable place at which to stay."

I had some difficulty in doing so, but returned in five or ten minutes saying it seemed "Hobson's choice" between two hotels, so we decided to go to the one that had a "runner" waiting to take care of our luggage.

The delay caused by seeking information about hotels brought us to the station office door just at the same moment that another traveler reached it. He touched me on the shoulder, saying, "Isn't this Brother McKay?"

Astonished beyond expression to be thus addressed in so strange a town, I turned and recognized Elder Wilford Booth, the one man above all others whom we were most desirous of meeting. We had met, too, at the most opportune time and place. Having known nothing of our whereabouts, he had come from the western part of the world, hoping in his heart to meet us. Knowing from the cablegram only that he was en route to Syria, we had come from the eastern part of the world, traveling westward, praying that we might meet him; and there we had met at the very time and place best suited to our convenience and to the success of our mission to the Armenians. It could not have been better had we been planning it for weeks!

As we recounted to each other our experiences, we had no doubt that our coming together was the result of divine interposition. If Brother Cannon and I had taken an auto from Jerusalem to Haifa; or if we had remembered to secure the name of a hotel before we left the Allenby, or if we had thought to ask the hotel runner at Ludd, we should not have met Elder Booth at Haifa. It is true he would have been in town that same day, but he was intending to stop at the German Hospice, where we should never have met him. He would have left by auto to Beirut; we, by train to Damascus.

Later developments showed that he would have been delayed at Beirut, while we should have been making fruitless search in Aleppo for the lost Saints.

Indeed, had it not been for our having met at Haifa, our trip to the Armenian Mission would have been, so far as human wisdom can tell, a total failure. As it was, among many duties and experiences, we organized the Armenian Mission, to take the place of the Turkish Mission.

This is only one incident of many which I might relate which have convinced me that if men will but seek the Lord in the right way, they will always find him. Truly, I can say with Benjamin Franklin, who evidently discovered the same truth: "The longer I live, the more convincing proof I see that God governs in the affairs of men."

# Reflections from a World Tour

*From an address delivered at the 92nd annual conference of the Church, Salt Lake Tabernacle, April 6, 1922.*

When President Hugh J. Cannon and I left home, December 4, 1920, we looked forward with no little misgiving and anxiety to the trip ahead of us. It was no simple matter to contemplate traveling to the Orient, thence to the Antipodes, much of that distance to be spent on the water. The distance itself made us realize that we were undertaking a great responsibility. Absence from our loved ones was keenly felt by both, but greater than these two, and other incidental things that made us hesitate about accepting this responsibility, was the realization that we were going on a first visit to our people to represent the General Authorities. The keen sense of our responsibility to fulfill adequately the desires of President Heber J. Grant and his counselors and the Twelve who had honored us with that call made us seek the Lord as I had never sought him before in my life, and I wish to say this afternoon that the promise made by Moses to the children of Israel just before they crossed the Jordan River into the Promised Land has been fulfilled in our experiences. As we sought the Lord with all our souls, he came to our guidance and assistance.

It may be that the realization of our dependence upon him made more prominent what seems to me to be a deplorable tendency of the world to disregard, even to disown, their relationship to our Heavenly Father. It was our privilege to hear educators and other prominent men speak in different places and upon different occasions, and to mingle with different classes of men and women on boats, for we spent a total of five months on the water, sailing in about twenty-three different vessels, every vessel well-crowded with all classes of tourists, most of whom were professional Christians. Frequently, we were grieved to note the attitude of apology that these Christian men and women assumed toward God, their Creator, and his Son, Jesus Christ.

I have been in mixed gatherings here in the state, and out of

Elders David O. McKay and Hugh J. Cannon at the Sphinx and the
Pyramids of Egypt, October 26, 1921.

the state, in which some men, when speaking of the early pioneers of Utah, would refer in a rather apologetic way to Brigham Young, and on some occasions I have felt that the speakers even hesitated to name him and give him the credit due him in the settlement of this great intermountain commonwealth, and in the founding of institutions that since have become centers of influence and might. Just such an attitude I have seen manifest among so-called Christians when they would begin to talk about God. He did not seem to be real to them. He did not seem to be in very deed their Father in heaven.

There is a tendency, it seems to me, among Christian nations to move toward a conception of God very much similar to the conception of the Buddhist who says, "There is no personal God-Creator on whose mercy and good will the universe is dependent. Everything owes its origin and development to its own inherent vitalism, or, what comes to the same, to its own will to live. Human ignorance it is which alone invented a personal God-Creator." The Buddhist utterly rejects the belief in a personal God. So do many in the Christian world. In opposition to this false conception of God, I wish to declare that today I feel as I have never felt before in all my life that God is my Father. He is not just an intangible power, a moral force in the world, but a personal God with creative powers, the Governor of the world, the Director of our souls. I should like to have the young men of Israel feel so close to him that they will approach him daily, not in public alone, but in private.

It is not imagination that we can approach God and can receive light and guidance from him, that our minds will be enlightened, our souls thrilled by his Spirit. Washington sought it; Abraham Lincoln received it; Joseph Smith knew it; and the testimony, the evidence of the Prophet Joseph's inspiration is manifest to all who will but open their eyes to see and their hearts to understand.

Inspiration was given to us on our world tour of the missions of the Church.

I want to testify to you that God was with us when we stood beneath that tree in old China when we dedicated that land to the preaching of the gospel. My words may not convince you of the fact, but no disputant can convince me that our souls were not filled to overflowing with the Spirit of God on that occasion.

Again the veil was thin between us and departed friends when we stood in prayer on the side of old Haleakala, the largest extinct volcano in the world, and poured our thanksgiving to God for what he had done for President Joseph F. Smith, George Q. Cannon, Elders Francis A. Hammond, James Hawkins, and their wives, and other missionaries who carried the gospel message to the Hawaiian people.

I knew of his protecting care in the Tongan Islands, for when the vessel was submerged by a mountainous wave, we felt peace and security.

At Papeete, Tahiti, we knew his guiding hand and acknowledged his overruling Providence when, replacing our judgment by his inspiration, he moved us to do something which our own judgment had told us not to do, subsequent events proving that the inspiration came in rich abundance in the priesthood meetings with the missionaries. God bless them wherever they are today, for they are God's servants as long as they will keep themselves pure and spotless from the sins of the world, and I testify to you that his Spirit is guiding them, magnifying them in their youth, making them a power in preaching the gospel of Jesus Christ.

Again, when among the Samoans, we felt his presence on several occasions, especially in that memorable farewell at Sauniatu.

Another memorable example of God's guiding hand was experienced when we met Joseph Wilford Booth at the very time and place that we should have met him in order to make our mission to the Armenians successful. I am convinced that there was some power above chance that brought about that meeting.

I desire to say to the children of Israel, in these valleys of the mountains, to the boys and girls especially: If you only knew that Christ is ever ready to give you help in time of need, and comfort and strength, you would approach him in purity, simplicity, and faith. May I illustrate it by the following poem:

> *The builder who first bridged Niagara's gorge,*
> *Before he swung his cable, shore to shore,*

*Sent out, across the gulf, his venturing kite*
*Bearing a slender cord for unseen hands*
*To grasp upon the further cliff, and draw*
*A greater cord, and a greater yet;*
*Till at last across the chasm swung*
*The cable—then a mighty bridge in air!*
*So we may send our little timid thought*
*Across the void, out to God's reaching hands—*
*Send out our love and faith to thread the deep—*
*Thought after thought, until the little cord*
*Has greatened to a chain no chance to break,*
*And we are anchored to the Infinite!*

—Edwin Markham

God bless our youth that they may send out these thoughts in prayer and faith and receive the assurance that they are anchored to the infinite.


# 'To See the Prophet''

*President Harold L. Gregory of the East German Mission relates an interesting incident of the chance meeting of two Russian war prisoners with President McKay during his visit to Berlin to dedicate the Charlottenburg chapel on June 28, 1952.*

June 16, 1954

Dear President McKay:

You will be interested to hear of an experience I had this week. Two men about forty years of age, poorly dressed, came to see me during the week. They told me they had lost their faith, and yet they could not turn to any of the other sects or religious organizations they knew. Mr. Braun (as one was called) had prevailed upon his friend, Mr. Fascher, to come and see me. He told Mr. Fascher that he knew of our church and that we would help them. Fascher objected strenuously for two days, but finally came along.

Mr. Braun began by saying that he was standing on a street corner one day when he noticed hundreds of people going by. He asked one where he was going, and he said, "To see the Prophet." Mr. Braun went along. It was the dedication of the meetinghouse in

Berlin-Charlottenburg, and the Prophet was Brother McKay.

He said (and I will quote him roughly): "I had never sensed such a spirit of love and good will as I did among those people that day. And then the Prophet, a tall man in his eighties, with a full head of hair—all white—stood up and addressed the body. I have never seen such a young face on a man that age. When he spoke, something went through me. Afterwards as he was getting into his car, I noticed he was shaking hands with the members, and even though I was not one of them I pressed forward and shook his hand too. Something warm and lovely went clear through my body, and I marveled again at his young, clear features. Through worldly cares and extreme economic difficulties the memory was somewhat beclouded, but I knew that I had to come back to find out more."

Mr. Fascher told me that Braun could say nothing but words of amazement and wonderment at the man he had seen. The two sat in my office and listened intently to the message of the restoration which I gave them, as if hanging on every word. They were penniless and miserable, but they were humble and dissatisfied with the churches of men. I lent them a Book of Mormon, and they promised to be to church Sunday. I believe these two men (both Russian war prisoners) are ready for the gospel.

May the Lord bless you, Brother McKay. You and all our brethren at the head of our church are shining examples of all that is righteous and good.

Sincerely your brother,
/signed/Harold L. Gregory

# "Something Unusual Happened This Day!"

---

*January 5, 1955, President and Sister McKay were aboard "The Clipper" on the first lap of their 45,000-mile trip to the South Sea island missions. President Franklin J. Murdock of the Highland Stake, who accompanied President and Sister McKay as traveling secretary, recorded the following incident in the day-by-day journal of this historic journey.*

At 3 A.M. (January 5, 1955) "The Clipper" stopped at Canton Island for refueling. How the pilots can find this small speck of coral just about a mile wide and six miles long in all of that huge Pacific Ocean is a wonder to me. We were delayed here three hours because of warnings that a hurricane was coming north from Suva. The hurricane turned around in its path and started south toward Suva again, but by the time we arrived it had abruptly changed its course and was going eastward, making our landing at Nandi safe and without incident. The black flags, which are the final warnings, were still flying as we landed, but the hurricane was well on its way north and eastward from Suva.

The officials at Nandi and Suva were puzzled to see the hurricane take such a course. I accompanied President McKay to the cable office, and the official there showed us the path of the hurricane and how it had suddenly reversed its course. It was thrilling to note that its pathway was timed to coincide with our arrival at Suva. President McKay remarked in the presence of the official at the cable office, "Something very unusual happened this day!"

We arrived at the Grand Pacific Hotel at 5:30 P.M., thankful and grateful to be there safe and sound.

*The* Daily News *of Suva, Fiji, carried the following headline on January 7, 1955: "HURRICANE. The all-clear has now been announced, and warnings withdrawn. The hurricane is moving away from Fiji to the southwest."*

*On Friday, January 7, 1955, President McKay noted in his personal diary the following: "Ray and I went up town to do a little shopping—met by accident Elder Boyd L. Harris, Stavely, Alberta, Canada, and Elder Sheldon L. Abbott, Mesquite, Nevada, also Brother C. G. Smith, a local elder, who has held the few members of the Church together here in Suva." (The missionaries, recognizing President McKay on the street, had stopped him.)*

*Up to this point President McKay was unaware that there were missionaries or members of the Church residing in Suva, and no arrangements had been made for a meeting. However, as soon as he learned at this chance meeting that there were members of the Church on the island, he immediately set aside a time for the holding of a meeting.*

Four days later, Sunday, January 9, 1955, President and Sister McKay attended a sacrament meeting at the home of Brother Cecil B. Smith, located on the outskirts of Suva, Fiji. Twenty-eight members of the Church were assembled, awaiting the arrival of the

President and his party. As they entered, Brother Smith came forward to welcome the visitors to his home. For thirty-three years he had kept this little flock together, and now the Prophet of the Lord and his wife were sitting in his home! It was too much for Brother Smith, and he broke down and wept tears of joy and thanksgiving. This humble man was so touched that he had some difficulty in leading the meeting. Then the congregation sang "We Thank Thee, O God, for a Prophet." Never was that song sung with such feeling and humility! With tears of joy in their eyes, they said every word as if it were a prayer.

Then President McKay stood up to talk to them. He pointed out that the meeting being held that day was very significant and of historical importance. There had been no intention of remaining in Suva over Sunday because the planned schedule of travel called for the McKay party to be somewhere between Suva and Tonga, but because of hurricane warnings, they were delayed a whole day. They were not aware that there were members of the Church in Suva. President McKay pointed out that thirty-four years ago Elder Hugh J. Cannon and he had stopped at Suva on the *SS Tofua,* but had decided that the time was not ripe for the preaching of the gospel to the people of Fiji. But on this day, Sunday, January 9, 1955, because of a change in their schedule which came about by reason of the hurricane warnings, they were here to preach the gospel in Suva and to commence the building up of the kingdom of God. President McKay then said: *"Surely God has had a hand in changing our schedule so that we can be with you, the members of the Church here on this island."* He told them that the eyes of the people of the island would be upon them, and that they must have good thoughts and render good deeds. He said that every member should be a missionary and urged all to work together for the acquiring of land upon which to build a chapel. He promised that if they would be faithful, they would have peace of mind, their faith would be increased, and their testimonies would be strengthened. He blessed them that peace might be in their hearts and in their homes with their families, and urged them all to work unitedly for the spreading of the gospel.

Following the meeting a dinner of native dishes was served to all the members. As they were gathered around the table, it was brought to their attention that one of the boys, now a grown man, and a woman, then a girl, had been on the ship with President McKay and Elder Hugh J. Cannon thirty-four years ago from Tonga to Hapaai where they had encountered a very severe storm. They described how high the waves were and how rough the sea, and that they had appealed to Apostle McKay, and he had offered a word of prayer, following which not only the waves had subsided, but also the sea had become calm.

# On the Hillside
# of Haleakala

*On Thursday, February 10, 1955, an informal meeting was held at Pulehu, Maui, Hawaii, on the site of the monument commemorating the place where the first baptisms in Hawaii had occurred and the first branch of the Church in the Hawaiian islands had been organized in 1851. President McKay and Elder Hugh J. Cannon had visited this site during their world tour of missions in 1921. At the meeting there in 1955, forty-four persons were present, including President and Sister McKay, Elder Clifford E. Young, President Franklin J. Murdock, officials of the Oahu Stake and the Hawaii Mission, and Saints in Hawaii. President McKay related the following experience.*

Brother Hugh J. Cannon had heard his father, President George Q. Cannon, tell of his visit to Wailuku, and of the remarkable manner in which he met Judge J. H. Napela. It was during a very wet season that he told the people he was making a tour of the island of Maui. They thought it a great undertaking and tried to persuade him not to go. However, he insisted upon going, and passed through a number of villages, over very rough, hilly country. Late one night he reached the town of Wailuku. Up to this time he had not met with the persons whom he had been led to expect, by the manifestations of the Spirit, who would receive his testimony concerning the gospel.

The main part of the town of Wailuku was on the other side of a stream, and in attempting to cross it, he became wet. There were some missionaries of other churches living at this place, and Brother Cannon hoped that he would get an opportunity to be introduced to them, for he had made it a rule not to pass a missionary without bearing testimony to him regarding his mission, but he was dusty and toil-worn and felt some diffidence about introducing himself.

By this time he had partly come to the conclusion that, as the weather was so unfavorable, he would return to Lahaina; and in passing through Wailuku he took a road which he thought led in that direction. He was scarcely out of town when he felt impressed to return, the Spirit telling him that if he would do so, he would have an opportunity of being introduced to the missionary who resided there.

As he passed the churchyard, two women emerged from a house nearby. When they saw Brother Cannon, they called to some men who were in the house, *"Eia ka haole,"* which means "Oh, the white man!" This they repeated two or three times, calling at the same time one of the men by name.

Elder George Q. Cannon, in recording this incident, wrote: "I was led to expect, before I left Lahaina, that I would find those who would receive me. Up to the time I reached Wailuku, I had not found them, and then when I thought it best to go back by another road, and through other villages, to Lahaina, I was told if I would return to Wailuku that I should obtain my desire in getting an interview with the missionary.

"The half-white women who saw me were Napela's wife and her sister. There was something very remarkable in their crying out as they did to him and his companions in the house when they saw me. They met whites very frequently, and it was nothing strange for them to pass as I did. This was often alluded to in conversations which we had afterwards, and they wondered why they should have done so. I know that it was the Lord's doings; for if they had not called out, I should have passed unnoticed and missed them. To my sight, the Lord's hand was plainly visible in it all, and I thanked him for his mercy and goodness."

As Brother Cannon walked to the picket fence, three men came out of the house and stepped up toward the gate. When Brother Cannon was opposite them, he saluted them, being greeted by them in return. The leader of the men invited Brother Cannon to stay with them until Monday. When he learned that he was a missionary, his desire to have him stay was increased.

The moment Brother Cannon entered into the house of this native and saw him and his two friends, he felt convinced that he had met the men for whom he had been looking.

The man who owned the house was a judge, and a leading man in that section. His name was Jonatana H. Napela. Judge Napela was very anxious to know Brother Cannon's belief and wherein the doctrines of the Church differed from the beliefs taught by the missionaries who were in their midst.

The opposition to the missionaries was very severe at first, but the judge stood up and defended them on every occasion.

About the middle of June 1851, a native house was built in the Kula country by Napela and his friends in which Elder Cannon held meetings. Elder Cannon held a meeting on July 23, 1851, after which 129 people were baptized.

Brother George Q. Cannon had told this story to Hugh J. Cannon, and when we visited Maui, Brother Hugh J. Cannon said, "I should like to go up to Pulehu." I said, "So should I." That was thirty-four years and two days ago. So we came up here, and this is where I was [pointing to a spot where a pepper tree had been], and as we looked at an old frame house that stood here then, he said, "That is probably the old chapel." It seemed to me it was over in the distance. Nothing else was here. We said, "Well, probably that is the place. We are probably standing on the spot upon which your father, George Q. Cannon, and Judge Napela addressed those people." We became very much impressed with the surroundings, association, and spiritual significance of the occasion, as we had also been with the manifestations we had had on our trip to the Orient and thus far in Hawaii. I said, "I think we should have a word of prayer." It was a hot day and the sun was shining, so we retired to the shade of a pepper tree that stood right on this spot. I should like to show you just how we stood. [President McKay lined up some of the brethren present as follows, reading from right to left: President Franklin J. Murdock, representing David Keola Kailimai, Elder Clifford E. Young as E. Wesley Smith, President McKay as himself, J. Pia Cockett as Hugh J. Cannon, and Dr. Reuben D. Law as Samuel Hurst.]

I offered the prayer. We all had our eyes closed, and it was a very inspirational gathering. As we started to walk away at the conclusion of the prayer, Brother Keola Kailimai took Brother E. Wesley Smith to the side and very earnestly began talking to him in Hawaiian. As we walked along, the rest of us dropped back. They continued walking, and Brother Kailimai very seriously told in Hawaiian what he had seen during that prayer. They stopped right over there [pointing a short distance away] and Brother E. Wesley Smith said, "Brother McKay, do you know what Brother Kailimai has told me?" I answered, "No." "Brother Kailimai said that while you were praying, and we all had our eyes closed, he saw two men who he thought were Hugh J. Cannon and E. Wesley Smith step out of line in front of us and shake hands with someone, and he wondered why Brother Cannon and Brother Smith were shaking hands while we were praying. He opened his eyes, and there stood those two men still in line, with their eyes closed just as they had been. He quickly closed his eyes because he knew he had seen a vision."

Now Brother Hugh J. Cannon greatly resembled Brother George Q. Cannon, his father. I spoke during our trip of his resemblance. Of course, E. Wesley Smith has the Smith attribute just as President Joseph Fielding Smith has it. Naturally, Brother Keola Kailimai would think that these two men were there. I said, "I think it was George Q. Cannon and Joseph F. Smith, two former missionaries to Hawaii, whom that spiritual-minded man saw."

We walked a few steps further, and I said, "Brother Kailimai, I do not understand the significance of your vision, but I do know that the veil between us and those former missionaries was very thin." Brother Hugh J. Cannon, who was by my side, with tears rolling down his cheeks, said, *"Brother McKay, there was no veil."*

There you have it. I am happy to be on this spot again.

The Lord is pleased with what the missionaries have done, and I am grateful for the response of the Hawaiian people and others of these lovely islands. I am glad to see this choice group of elders and members here assembled, for this truly is a sacred spot. May we who will now have increased responsibility from this moment on be true to the trust that the Lord has in us!

# Section III

## Faith-
## Promoting
## Experiences

# A Photographer Finds a Prophet of God

*Arch L. Madsen, president of KSL Radio and Television, related this incident to the students of Brigham Young University, and it was later published in the September 1963 issue of* The Improvement Era.

Recently in New York an experience occurred that a friend of mine at the United Press passed along. When President McKay came home from Europe, arrangements had been made for his picture to be taken. The regular photographer assigned was unable to go to Idlewild [now John F. Kennedy Airport] and so, in desperation, the United Press picked the man assigned to take President McKay's picture who was their crime photographer—a man accustomed to the very toughest type of work in New York.

This man went to the airport and came back in due time, went into the darkroom to develop his pictures, and stayed almost two hours. When he came out, he had a tremendous sheaf of pictures in his hand. He was supposed to take only two pictures. His boss immediately chided him and said, "What in the world are you wasting time and all those photographic supplies for?"

The boss received a very curt and sharp answer. The crime photographer would gladly pay for the extra materials he had used; they could dock him for the hours he had spent on this work, because these extra pictures were his own personal property.

It was obvious at the time he was very touchy on the subject. Several hours later the vice-president of United Press called him in to learn what had happened. This in essence is the story the crime photographer gave him:

"You see, when I was a little boy, my mother used to read to me out of the Old Testament a great deal. I loved the stories about God's prophets, and I have wondered all my life what a prophet of God must really look like. Well, today, I found one!"

# Man's Extremity Is God's Opportunity

*President McKay relates an experience that occurred when he was presiding over the Scottish Conference in Glasgow, Scotland, in 1897-99.*

There is an old saying that "man's extremity is God's opportunity." You remember the story I have told about James L. McMurrin of the European Mission presidency, who had to fill an appointment in Falkirk, Scotland, on Sunday. He was in Burntisland Saturday night and he had a sixpence or a shilling in his pocket to pay for his boat ride across the Leith Walk to Edinburgh. When that was spent, he had no more money and was alone. The only way he could get to Falkirk was by the one train that was then running between Edinburgh and Glasgow.

He had an appointment with the branch in Edinburgh from ten to twelve. He filled that appointment. When they asked him to go to lunch, he said, "No, thank you, I have to be in Falkirk and I have to take the train that leaves at one o'clock." One by one the Saints bade him goodbye, all but Brother Robertson, who was president of the branch. He said, "Well, if ye canna go hame with me, I'll gae ye a Scotch convoy," and together they walked across Princes Street and down to Waverly Station, crossing under the glass-covered canopy over to the gate from which the train was to leave.

The only possible way that Brother McMurrin could have kept his appointment that night was to get that train. He had faith that the Lord would open the way. He did not ask anyone for a shilling, nor for a sixpence, nor for twopence, nor for two and six. As the time approached, Brother Robertson said, "Well, Brother McMurrin, it is time just to get your ticket, so I shall say good-bye." "Goodbye, Brother Robertson," answered Brother McMurrin, and he was left alone. There was his extremity.

"Father" (and I shall give you his words of prayer as he gave them to me), "Father, I have come just as far as I can in fulfilling my duty. Open up the way that I may get on this train and go to

Falkirk." He had in mind, President McMurrin said, that the gate-keeper would probably let him go through. He did not think of the fact that the gatekeeper was a Scotsman and that he would never do that. What happened? Brother Robertson, who left Brother Mc-Murrin a few moments before, had just returned to the steps leading up to Princes Street, and the thought suddenly came to him, "I wonder if Brother McMurrin has enough money to get on that train!" Quickly retracing his steps, he walked across the station, pulled out of his pocket a two and sixpence, ran over to where Brother McMurrin was, and said, "Here, Brother McMurrin, perhaps you need this." "Thank you, Brother Robertson, I needed that money to get my ticket."

Man's extremity is God's opportunity!

Someday you in the Church will come against a wall. It may seem to be across your path. It may be a moral wall and you cannot overcome it, or you cannot get through it; you cannot see. But you can walk from here to that wall, having faith that God will give you a ladder, or show you a hidden ladder or an opening; and he will do it if you will walk just as far as you can in the performance of your duty. No matter what it is or how difficult your duty, do it; walk that distance and then say in all sincerity and faith, "Father, help me; open up the way that I may do my duty," and he will do it.

# Lessons from Life

*Excerpts from an address given at the 26th annual convention of the Primary Association, June 1928.*

You have little children who come to you tainted with profanity. Teach them to reverence God and his laws, to speak well of them, to speak well of his priesthood. That spirit inculcated in the minds and hearts of little children will lead them to God as no other spirit will.

Sisters, give your life for the little ones and you will save it, not only in the memory of childhood, which is sweet, a salvation worthy to be sought after; but you will also save your soul in the presence of Christ. I promise you that. Devote your energy to putting these ethical principles in the minds of the children.

What do I want my boy to be? I want him to be honest; I want him to have faith in God and faith in his priesthood; I want him to pray night and morning; I want him to eschew evil things; I do not want him to tell vulgar stories; I do not want him to do poor things in a poor way; I want him to love his teacher as he loves his mother. And you want your children to do the same. God bless you in your efforts to do it.

I testify to you that there are those on the other side who will help you in this work. Is there a mother you have lost? She is ready to help you. Is there a father? He is there. Those who presided over this association and who labored with the young before and after the Primary Association was organized are ready to help you. I have been thinking of Sister Eliza R. Snow today and the impression she made upon me as a little boy; I have been thinking of Sister Moselle Hall and her associates, some of whom are on the other side, who taught Primary many years; how their influence remains! But my thought at this moment is particularly for those who have gone beyond; I testify to you this morning that their influence can be felt in church work today.

I believe that those you love, especially those who have gone beyond, and especially Christ, your Redeemer, stand by you as you give yourself for these little ones.

# The Value of Counsel

*From an address given by President McKay at Fresno, California, May 18, 1952.*

Men sit in council, but the value of that council is for each one to express what he feels, independently of whether it is going to please somebody else or not. That is the value of counsel, and associated with that is the ability to yield that independent thought to the thought of the group—three members of a bishopric sitting there counseling, each one giving his best thought, his best judgment, and even the inspiration that comes to him. But when the two decide, then the other says, "That becomes my view with yours."

I saw it in a council meeting one day when a question of grave importance came up. I was in harmony with my president in the council, President Francis M. Lyman, and with other members of that council, and we were united as we met with the First Presidency that morning.

President Joseph F. Smith did not ask our view that day. Usually he asked the junior member to express his thoughts and give his best judgment. To our surprise, the President did not ask that. He arose and said, "This is what the Lord wants."

While it was not wholly in harmony with what we had decided, President Lyman, the president of the Twelve, was the first on his feet. "Brethren," he said, "I move that that become the opinion and judgment of this council."

"I second the motion," said another, and it was unanimous. Six months did not pass before the wisdom of that leader was demonstrated.

Think independently, but be united with the majority of your associates in council.

# A Distinctive People

*From an address delivered by President McKay at a seminary youth conference in the Rexburg (Idaho) Tabernacle May 3, 1947.*

Our debt to our forebears and parents is unpayable, except in one way: that is in emulating their ideals and bringing joy to them in their old age, and bringing satisfaction to those who have gone before by keeping ourselves clean and wholesome.

But we have a responsibility to honor their names and to honor the Church for another reason. There is something distinctive about this people. You often hear it said we are a peculiar people, quoting Peter of old. Perhaps we are. I don't like the word *peculiar* so much as I do that we are *distinctive* people.

Recently I have been deeply impressed with the fact that people outside our church somehow become convinced or impressed with that distinctiveness, and in emphasizing our responsibility, may I call your attention to a few of these things which have come to my personal attention. A few years ago Gordon S. Rentschler, chairman of the board of the National City Bank in New York, was given a dinner by Orval W. Adams, a prominent Utah businessman. It was a very distinguished affair, at the conclusion of which Mr. Rentschler arose to express his appreciation. This is what he said:

"One of my first experiences in Utah was twenty odd years ago when Orville Wright and I came here one day with four or five others. We went over to the temple grounds and were taken around by a man whose name we never learned. He was an extraordinary individual. Afterwards Orville Wright and I went back to the Hotel Utah and Orville said, 'You know, that fellow has got something that we are all missing, and that is the reason the Mormons are great people!' "

Some time later, we were at another dinner at the Hotel Utah, given by the board of directors of the United States Steel Company, thirteen of whom had come to visit Salt Lake City and the steel plant in Orem. They had invited the First Presidency of the Church and some of the General Authorities to be their guests at the dinner.

At the conclusion of the dinner, Nathan L. Miller, formerly governor of New York State and then director and general council for the United States Steel Corporation, arose and said, "I would like to say something in appreciation of the cordiality extended to the directors of the United States Steel Company while in this city and visiting the Geneva Steel plant. I am one of those New Englanders who have harbored all the ill stories that have been circulated about the Mormons, but I will confess that this visit has extended my horizon." Then he added, "No one can walk or drive around this city, observe its cleanliness, its wide, well-kept streets, the physical accomplishments evident on every hand, without being impressed with a feeling that there is something peculiar and distinctive here, something different from that felt in any other city. I don't know whether to call it spirituality. Yes, that's it. There is evidence of spirituality, the lack of which is felt in other cities."

He said he had been searching for the source of it but could not find that source until he heard the tribute paid to the pioneers during a brief interview in the office of the First Presidency. "There was a great ideal, a greatness among the founders of Utah. Your very isolation has been a contributing factor in helping the pioneers to maintain the high standards that characterize the lives of the founders of this state."

Just a month or so ago, I met the president of a rubber company that is building a two-million-dollar plant in Nephi, Utah. He tore one down in California, laid it to the ground after having bought it, because of labor trouble. We were invited to Nephi to a dinner given for stake presidencies and bishops and others in that area. I accepted the invitation because I wondered why that company was spending two million dollars in a state that could give no national profit for the production of that rubber.

That's the first time I met the company president, a very choice man. I was deeply impressed with his high standards and ideals. I said to him, among other things, "Will you tell me why you are spending this money to build that plant here in this western country?" He said, "I am going to answer that tonight." And he did. The one outstanding reason for that company's building that plant is because of the confidence that he and his associates have in the integrity and personality of the men and women of Utah. I remember, when asked to respond, that I said to those men, "If that is the only reason for the company's coming here to invest their funds, then there is a great responsibility upon us so to live to merit their confidence."

Let me give you one more example. Leo Tolstoy was a great writer, a great thinker. One day an ambassador attacked the Mormons in Count Tolstoy's presence, and this is reported as what that great writer and thinker said: "Dr. White, I am greatly surprised and disappointed that a man of your great learning and position should be so ignorant on this important subject. They teach the American religion. Their principles teach the people not only of heaven and its attendant glories, but how to live so that their social and economic relations with each other are placed on a sound basis. If the people follow the teachings of this church, nothing can stop their progress. It will be limitless. There have been great movements started in the past, but they have died or have been multiplied before they reached maturity. If Mormonism is able to endure, unmodified, until it reaches the third and fourth generation, it is destined to become the greatest power the world has ever known."

Your responsibility and mine is to keep unmodified and unpolluted. It will be only a few years before the responsibilities now carried by some of us will be on your shoulders. You cannot afford to waste or blight your youth!

# Insidious Influences on the Inside

*From remarks made by President McKay at the Liverpool Conference in Burnley, England, March 30, 1924.*

One evening down in Samoa, the mission president and I stood up on the second story of a schoolhouse belonging to the Church, where 150 or perhaps 200 little children studied under elders who were devoting their whole time free of charge. Service! But that is incidental. We were inspecting the building to make it more comfortable and safer for those little tots who were sitting on the ground learning their lessons from the books and blackboards with which we could furnish them. I walked up to a railing that I thought was quite solid, and I was surprised when I barely leaned against it to have the entire railing fall to the ground. "There," said the mission president, "that is it. The whole building, Brother McKay, is just that way." "Well," I said, "it looks solid," and it *was* solid on the outside, but it was fairly eaten up within by millions of white ants or termites that had buried themselves inside. The outside looked perfect, but inside it was gone.

There are many little things in life that, like that white ant, burrow themselves into the soul and undermine the character.

# The Way Is
# Open to the Spirit

*From an address by President McKay to missionaries of the North British Mission in Manchester, England, March 1, 1961.*

One day in Glasgow when the weight of the responsibilities of the presidency of the Glasgow Conference was upon my young shoulders, there was trouble in the branch. Two of the brethren began to fight—not physically, but calling each other names. It began in the Sunday School class in the morning between one brilliant man, Brother Leggatt, whom I learned to love, and another brother who was a converted minister, a Brother Clark.

Brother Leggatt gave a wonderful explanation of a passage in the Old Testament, "I am that I am," and he analyzed it thus: "I am that being associated with the word *be* (*am* is *be*) and Being means 'always existed.' 'I am that I am therefore means 'I am that always existed.' "

Brother Clark said, "Oh, yes, I knew that." Brother Leggatt, in his Scottish accent said, "No, ya dinna." "Yes, I did." "No, ya did not—you didn't." And they quarreled right there in the class and upset the whole Sunday School. Brother Clark then picked up his hat and said, "I'll leave the room and I'll never come back here as long as that man is in the presidency of the branch." Dissension in the branch—a condition that is not very easy to meet!

That was a test. I heard a voice that I had prayed for as a youth. The inspiration came to me what to do to settle this dispute between these men to bring about unity in the branch and further the work of the Lord without such antagonisms. There was a great deal more associated with this incident that I need not mention. I heard the voice and got in touch with the Spirit as never before. My prayer was answered, not in the way I had anticipated, but in the way the Lord intended it to be answered. That was the beginning of the revelation of the Spirit to my soul.

Part of that incident came the next day when I called to see Brother Leggatt across the River Clyde, and it was completed when

Brother Leggatt said, "I'll gae [give] you a Scot's convoy." He walked with me up to the bridge across the railroad track. I said, "Brother Leggatt, you were not to blame for that incident Sunday morning. Brother Clark should ask your forgiveness—at least he should come halfway—but I am going to ask you to go all the way and ask Brother Clark's forgiveness and settle the dispute between you. You two are leaders in this branch."

I shall never forget the moment that followed. I can even remember now his running his hand up through his hair and dropping his head. "It's gae [very] hard but I'll de [do] it." And he did. He went up to Springburn and entered Brother Clark's shop—he was a shoemaker. Brother Clark looked up and said, "Oh, it's you, is it?" Then he turned his back on Brother Leggatt and sat down, hammering at a shoe. Brother Leggatt was true to his promise and said, "I have come up to shake your hand and to ask your forgiveness for my part in that untoward incident before the entire church."

Brother Clark said, "Well, if you mean it," and Brother Leggatt walked out.

Later Brother Clark had a change of heart. He came down and asked Brother Leggat's forgiveness, and the next Sunday they went arm in arm to their Sunday School meeting. Rupture of an entire branch had been averted through the inspiration of the Lord on that Monday morning.

And now I stand before you today bearing testimony that the channel of communication is open, and the Lord is ready to guide, and does guide, his people. Is that not worth resisting temptation, just for the gratification of a whim or a passion?

So the way is open to the Spirit, to a testimony of the Spirit that is in harmony with the spirit of creation, the Holy Ghost. The Spirit of the Lord animates and enlivens every person in the Church or out of it. By him we live and move and have our being, but the testimony of the Holy Ghost is a special privilege. It is like tuning in the radio and hearing a voice on the other side of the world. Men who are not within that radiation cannot hear it, but we hear it, and we are entitled to that voice and the guidance of it. It will come to us if we do our part; but if we take the other pathway and yield to our own instincts, our own desires, our own passions, and we pride ourselves that we are thinking and planning and scheming, things will become dark. We will accomplish the gratification of our passions or our appetites, but we deny the Spirit and cut off the communication between our spirit and the Spirit of the Holy Ghost.

# A Temple in the South Seas

*The New Zealand Temple was dedicated by President McKay on April 20, 1958, on a site selected by him in early 1955. While he had been on his world tour of the missions in 1920-22, he had visited Sauniatu, Upolu, Samoa, and had predicted that a chapel would one day be built in that beautiful location. He returned to Sauniatu and dedicated a chapel there January 15, 1955, at which time he made the following remarks.*

You members of the Church should have an opportunity to do your temple work. As I envisioned thirty-four years ago what we have seen in reality in Sauniatu today, so I envision that someday there will be a temple in the south seas to which you and your children may go to receive the blessings of the House of the Lord. Just where it will be we cannot say this morning, but it will be nearer than Salt Lake City. For the first time in the history of the Church the General Authorities have approved a plan to build beautiful but inexpensive temples in various parts of the world, where the members of the Church may remain in their own branches and receive all the blessings that any other member of the Church may have. When that inspiration came to the President of the Church and he [President McKay] presented it to his counselors and the Council of the Twelve, they voted unanimously to establish that course throughout the world.

This year, on September 11, the first temple in Europe will be dedicated at Berne, Switzerland. About the same time the foundation of the London Temple will be laid at Newchapel, near London. In December, about the first week in December, the Los Angeles Temple, the largest ever built in this or any other dispensation, will be dedicated.

How is it possible to do these things and accomplish this great purpose of the Lord? Because the members of the Church are doing their duty. They are not merely saying, "Lord, Lord," but they are doing his will—praying, rendering service as missionaries, paying their tithes and offerings, and thus making it possible to give the blessings of the House of the Lord to all members of the Church.

*On January 13, 1955, President McKay delivered a speech in the Tongan Mission at which he said:*

Do you know what I saw today, in vision? A temple on one of these islands where the members of the Church may go and receive the blessings of the temple of God. You are entitled to it. We are not so far apart now. We used to think that the Saints in South Africa were way off on the other side of the globe, and geographically they are, but do you know that Sister McKay and I could leave Salt Lake City, fly across the Atlantic Ocean and down and across the Sahara Desert to our branch in South Africa in less time than it took President Brigham Young to go from Salt Lake City to St. George in Utah?

A week ago last Sunday, in a blinding snowstorm, we said goodbye to our loved ones at home. Next morning we were in San Francisco. We left there Tuesday morning and that night we were in Honolulu, Hawaii. And the next morning we were on Canton Island, and that evening in Suva, and if the hurricane hadn't frightened the sailors, we could have been with you two days earlier.

Now, I am mentioning that to say that one purpose of our visit here is to let you feel that you are part of the Church—an important part of the Church—and your welfare is very dear to the hearts of the First Presidency and the other General Authorities. I come in person this morning to give you their love and blessing.

# The Singing Missionaries

*An amusing incident of missionaries singing three songs to the same tune on the street corners in Scotland, 1897 to 1899, as told by President David O. McKay at a missionary banquet held in a hall at Scheveningen, Holland, June 13, 1952.*

Now, about music. I could never sing. I have never been blessed with that—I haven't an ear for music. Sister McKay has all that. When I entered the mission field, I entered with the memory of a failure in a quartet. We failed when we appeared in public. After that I didn't try. It was a mistake, and I suffered for it, as you will see. Fortunately, Archie Anderson, a young man about thirty years of age from Sanpete County, had been active in Glasgow and had been leader of the singing on the street corners. He had a good voice, and we joined him. But then he was released, so within a week or ten days after our arrival in Glasgow we were left on our own.

During our association with him, we learned three songs, and they are good street songs: "Israel, Israel, God Is Calling," "O My Father," and "What Was Witnessed in the Heavens?" We sang them in that order every night. "Israel, Israel, God Is Calling" was an appeal to people to come and listen. After the prayer, "O My Father" was an appeal for help. Then before we closed the meeting, we bore testimony to the restoration of the gospel, so it was highly appropriate to sing "What Was Witnessed in the Heavens?" And this is the way we sang them. Taking our place without any audience, we started out.

(President McKay sings:)

*Israel, Israel, God is calling,*
*Calling thee from lands of woe. . . .*

After the prayer,

(President McKay sings again to the tune of "Israel, Israel, God Is Calling")

*O my Father, thou that dwellest,*
*In that high and glorious place. . . .*

After the testimony, conclusion:

(President McKay sings again to the same tune of "Israel, Israel, God Is Calling")

*What was witnessed in the heavens?*
*Why an angel from on high.*

It made no difference—the repetition of the melodies—because we didn't have the same audience at the conclusion that we had at the beginning.

# A Portrait in the Pioneer Memorial Theatre

*President McKay was paid high tribute at unveiling ceremonies of his portrait at the Pioneer Memorial Theatre, University of Utah, on June 8, 1964. Dr. A. Ray Olpin, president of the university, said the following in a letter dated May 15, 1964.*

"This year, my last in office, we want to be a little special and honor you for the encouragement and help you have given us during your long service to the Church and community. You and Sister McKay have always been devoted patrons of the drama. We are mindful of the tremendous leadership you have displayed in getting the Pioneer Memorial Theatre campaign under way and the building completed. In order that your role in bringing to reality a suitable place for theatrical productions in this community and specifically on the campus of the University of Utah may be properly understood and appreciated by present and future generations, we plan to have a formal portrait of you hanging on the main wall of the majestic lobby of the Theatre."

At the ceremonies, Dr. Olpin said, "It is doubtful if the Pioneer Memorial Theatre would ever have been built without the help and inspiration of President McKay."

The plaque under the portrait reads: "David O. McKay, religious leader—educator—patron of the arts—prime mover in the creation of this building in memory of the Utah Pioneers who built the first theatre in the Rocky Mountains."

Dr. Olpin, in his talk when the portrait painting of President McKay was presented, told of the difficulties encountered in getting the State Legislature to approve of the appropriation for the Pioneer Memorial Theatre. He said it looked as though their dream might not materialize, so they decided to have a meeting of all the senators and legislators, the civic officials, and others in the Governor's Board Room. Dr. Olpin then said, "I will never forget as long as I live the change that came over the faces in that room filled to standing-room-only capacity of people, prominent people. As they arose, President McKay came in, and with that wonderful smile on his face, he walked over and stood before them and said: 'Gentlemen, I came to confess my sins.' That was all it took. Before we left there, everyone had pledged that the money would be appropriated; and I think the first item of business when the Legislature convened was to appropriate that half-million dollars so the Board of Examiners would not be found violating the law or the state constitution. It was for one thing after another of that kind that this man gave his support to us."

# Section IV

## Experiences of Divine Healing

# The Power of Healing

By Clare Middlemiss

President David O. McKay spent his life in traveling throughout the world to bless and encourage both members and nonmembers of the Church. Wherever he went, the people formed a veritable cordon about him, nor would they disperse until each had the opportunity to shake his hand. Many of the lands visited by him had never had an apostle of the Lord within their borders, and many of the people had a burning faith that if they could only grasp him by the hand, they would receive increased strength thereby. Their desire was increased by the fact that perhaps there would never be another opportunity in a lifetime to shake the hand of a chosen representative of the Lord. Between meetings, it was almost impossible for President McKay to take a needed rest, for all the people were desirous of receiving a blessing from him. All who came to him were greeted and blessed as sincerely and prayerfully as his soul could bless. There were perhaps hundreds who were healed through his administration, and thousands of others were blessed and encouraged by the warm clasp of his hand.

In an address given January 3, 1953, President McKay said: "Faith is operating today as it has always operated. Our Father in heaven is just as near now as he was when he stood by the Savior's side and appeared to the Prophet Joseph Smith."

The following incidents are given as a testimony that the power of healing is operative today through the priesthood properly bestowed upon the servants of the Lord. It will be noted that in nearly all of these cases, faith in the priesthood was operative in the individual who received the blessing.

# A Personal Experience of Divine Healing

*The following experience was dictated by President McKay July 10, 1945.*

In March 1916, Ogden River overflowed. It came through the Narrows a raging torrent.

Wednesday noon I drove three of my young children up there as far as the Narrows so that they might see the river at floodtide and hear the grinding of the stones as they pushed against each other by the force of the water.

Wednesday night my brother, Thomas E., called at the house. Unable to get through the canyon, he called his wife by telephone and asked if she would send a horse down with the road supervisor the next morning so that he (Thomas E.) might get up to the valley. As he hung up the telephone, he turned to my son Lawrence and said, "Will you please drive me up as far as where the road is washed out?" Having been up just that afternoon and knowing the danger, I said, "I think I had better drive you, Thomas E., if you will get up early in the morning so I can get back in time to catch my train for Salt Lake City."

The next morning several things delayed us, and it was seven o'clock before we started for the canyon. My train left in one hour. I hesitated for a moment, thinking that I should not have time to drive up to the mouth of the canyon and return by eight o'clock. It was then that I received a strong impression to *"go up to the bridge and back."*

We jumped into a little Ford car and dashed through the rain and mud up 21st Street toward the canyon road. Without my having said anything to Thomas E. about my impression, he said, "I think you had better not attempt to cross the bridge."

Notwithstanding these two warnings, as we approached the bridge I thought I could spend another five minutes and take him up as far as I had taken the children the day before. I saw the pile of rocks there at the bridge, and it seemed to be intact just as it had been the day before. So jocularly I said, "I'm going across the bridge. Can you swim?" With that I stepped on the gas and dashed across the bridge, only to hear Thomas E. say, "Oh, look out! There's a rope!" The watchman who left at seven o'clock had stretched the derrick rope across the road, and his successor, the day watchman, had not arrived. I reached for the emergency brake but was too late. The rope smashed the window, threw back the top, and caught me just in the chin, severing my lip, knocking out my lower teeth, and breaking my upper jaw. Thomas E. ducked his head and escaped uninjured, but I was left partially senseless.

The engine of the car was unimpaired, and Thomas E. moved me over in the seat, turned the car around, and drove toward home. Just as we neared the top of the hill on Canyon Road, I heard him say, "I think I had better take you to the hospital." I opened my eyes and saw blood in my hand and some loose broken teeth. I said, "No, you had better take me home. Something has happened."

About nine o'clock that morning I was on the operating table in care of Dr. Joseph R. Morrell and Dr. Robert S. Joyce. They sewed my upper jaw in place and took fourteen stitches in my lower lip and lacerated cheek.

One of the attendants remarked, "Too bad; he will be disfigured for life."

Certainly I was most unrecognizable. When I was wheeled back to my room in the hospital, one of the nurses consolingly remarked, "Well, Brother McKay, you can wear a beard," meaning that thus I might hide my scars.

Word of the accident soon spread throughout the city, and at ten o'clock that Thursday morning Bishop A. E. Olson, President Thomas B. Evans, and Heber Scowcroft, three very close friends, called and administered to me. In sealing the anointing, Bishop Olson said, "We bless you that you shall not be disfigured and that you shall not have pain."

Friday morning one of my dearest friends, Peter G. Johnston, came down from Blackfoot, Idaho. My face was so swollen and disfigured that he did not recognize me. He passed by the open door, thinking that I was the wrong patient. When he entered later and was leaving, he said, "Well, the eyes are the same anyhow."

Saturday evening Dr. William H. Petty called to see if the teeth that were still remaining in the upper jaw might be saved. It was he who said, "I suppose you are in great pain." I answered, "No, I haven't *any* pain." He said, "I cannot understand that—I should think that you would have neuralgia pains."

That evening I began to wonder whether or not my nerves were stunned. As I dozed, my arm that I evidently had up at my forehead dropped and hit some of the stitches on my face. Then I knew that my nerves were not stunned, as I felt the pain intensely, for I was aware of the contact of my hand on the stitches.

Sunday morning President Heber J. Grant came up from Salt Lake City. He was then President of the Council of the Twelve. Having noticed the sign on the door, "Visitors Not Allowed," he entered and said, "David, don't talk; I'm just going to give you a blessing."

Among other things he said, "I bless you that you shall not be scarred." Later when he took his hands off my head and looked at me he thought (as he afterwards told me), "My, I've made a promise that cannot be fulfilled!"

On the following Monday morning the doctors removed the stitches from my lower lip, the severed parts having joined together. When Dr. Joyce came in Tuesday morning to take out the stitches from my face, he said, "Well, Mr. McKay, it pays to live a clean life!" Wednesday morning I returned home.

The following October, at a banquet given to the General Authorities on the Roof Garden of the Hotel Utah, I sat at a table near where President Grant was sitting. I noticed that he was looking at me somewhat intently, and then he said, "David, from where I am sitting I cannot see a scar on your face!" I answered, "No, President Grant, there are no scars—your blessing was realized completely."

# The Prayer
# of a Child

*Dictated by President McKay, August 1940.*

"Lord, teach us how to pray" was the reverent plea of the disciples of the Master. Humble as children, they sought proper guidance, and their appeal was not in vain.

Just as keenly as did the disciples sense this need, so at times may children sense the need of divine guidance and comfort, yet not express their yearning in spoken request. Hence the Lord has placed upon parents the duty to teach their children to pray.

Worries, perplexities, and sorrows are as real in the life of a little child as in the adult world, and children are entitled to the comfort, consolation, and guidance obtained from God through prayer.

Not only that, but from the standpoint of faith, sincerity, and abiding trust, the prayer of an innocent child will surely receive most ready response from a loving Father. Here is a true story of one such instance that brought almost immediate results.

William (not the boy's true name) was a lad who had been taught to pray. When he was about ten years old, his father was nearly killed in an automobile accident. It happened early in the morning, and so grief-stricken were the mother and children, including William, that none could eat a meal or cared to.

However, later in the day, after the doctors had sewed up the lacerations, repaired the broken bones, and given assurances that their daddy was not fatally injured, the loved ones calmed their fears and began to resume the regular family routine.

As was the practice in that Mormon home, before the evening meal, all knelt in prayer. Following it, William started away from the table. Seeing this his mother said, "Come, Will, sit down and eat your dinner."

"No, Mother," replied the lad, "I am not hungry."

"You must!" insisted the mother. "You haven't eaten all day.

Don't worry any longer, Daddy will be all right."

"Please excuse me, Mother. I am fasting and want to go up to my room."

He did go to his room, and there he knelt in earnest prayer for his father's speedy and complete recovery.

Rising from his knees, he put on his hat, picked from his little garden the few first violets of springtime, walked to the hospital, and placed the flowers in his injured father's hand. As the father received them, he recognized in the lad's face an expression that reflected the yearning of his little soul for his father's recovery. There was no need for words. Father and son understood each other, and the Lord comforted both—the boy in the consolation, the father in the assurance that the Lord would answer the lad's prayer.

And he did in a miraculously speedy and permanent recovery.

*The incident related above is a true story of the automobile accident in which President McKay was injured, and the child, William, who prayed for his father, is President McKay's own son.*

# Behind the Iron Curtain

On Sunday, June 29, 1952, Sister McKay and I were in Berlin, Germany, near the Iron Curtain. Arrangements had been made for a meeting of the Saints, investigators, and friends in the Mercedes Palast Theater, the largest hall in North Berlin.*

Prior to the meeting I had received word through the presidency of the East German Mission that one of the members of the Church in that mission, a sister, had lost her husband and eldest

---

*Note: At the meeting held in this hall a total of 2600 crowded into the building, filling the stage, aisles, the driveways, and every available space. The Berlin police force aided in keeping the large crowd orderly, and allowed members to stand and fill the aisles, a thing contrary to city ordinances. President McKay's subject was on the immortality of the soul, and he called on the nations of the earth for obedience to the gospel of Jesus Christ. Everyone present had an opportunity to shake hands with President McKay.

son under Communist rule. She had been driven from her home and was subsequently exposed to the rigors of the weather and lack of nutrition until she finally became paralyzed and had been confined to her bed for five years. She had heard of my coming to Berlin, and being unable to travel herself, she expressed the desire that her two little children—a boy and a girl about ten and twelve years of age—be sent over to meet the President of the Church. This good sister said, "I know if I send my children to shake hands with President McKay, and then they come home and take my hand—if I can hold their little hands in mine—I know that I shall get better."

Arrangements were made for them to take the trip. Some of the Saints contributed to the clothing of the little children, and the missionaries contributed to pay their expenses.

I asked the mission president to point out these little children as they came to the meeting. Two little children among thousands who were assembled! Anticipating meeting them, I took a new handkerchief, and when that little girl and boy came along, I went to them and shook their hands and said, "Will you take this handkerchief to your mother with my blessing?" I later learned that after I had shaken hands with them, they would not shake hands with anyone else, for they did not want to touch anyone with their hands until they got back to their mother.

We heard no more about it; however, the incident was well-known throughout the crowd. I saw the children again in the conference house that night. They were sleeping on the top floor of the mission home—sweet little darlings!

When Sister McKay returned to Salt Lake City, she wrote to the mission president's wife and asked her to find out how the mother of the two little children was getting along. In her reply, the mission president's wife wrote: "This sister thanks the Lord every day for the blessing and the handkerchief which President McKay sent through her two children, and she has faith that she will fully recover, and I believe so, too. Immediately after the children came home, her feet and toes began to get feeling in them, and this feeling slowly moved up into her legs, and now she gets out of bed alone and seats herself on a chair, and then, with her feet and the chair, works all the way around to the kitchen sink, where she has the children bring her the dishes to wash, and other things, and is very thankful that she is able to help now."

That is the faith of a mother in the Russian zone. God bless her, and bless all who are over there!

# A Member in Tonga

*The following letter was received in August 1938 from Elder William M. Waddoups, formerly president of the Hawaii Mission. It has reference to an incident that happened when President McKay was in the Tongan Islands in 1921.*

Dear President McKay:

Recently I have heard of a little incident containing much human interest in which I am sure you will have a very personal interest. I am writing it to you for two purposes: that you may know how the leaven is working in the islands of the sea, and may also see some of the many great blessings to the people that followed your visit to those islands a number of years ago.

There is now living in Neiafu Vavao Tonga a true Latter-day Saint by the name of John Kalusi.

Some time ago a great desire possessed him to get a clear understanding of his ancestral line and to obtain sufficient information concerning them to perform temple ordinances in their behalf. He had been told that a woman living in a nearby village was a relative of his family. He visited her, found her to be a relative, obtained some information, and was referred to another village where he would also find a relative. He obtained more information and was directed to visit a certain person in still another nearby village. There he learned that a prominent high chief of the village was his relative. He visited him and found in his possession a written record in longhand of his immediate ancestors back to the year A.D. 950. You may imagine his great joy.

Now comes the great human interest side of this family. The wife of John Kalusi, Vii by name, was childless. She had had several premature births and despaired of ever having a matured child. While you and President Hugh J. Cannon were visiting in Tonga, she asked you for a blessing that she might become the mother of a living child. In due course of time after the blessing, a well-developed son was born to her. He was given the the name of Mataili. He is now about seventeen years old. The father now has a son to help him in doing work for his numerous ancestral line in the House of the Lord.

With pleasure I report a great awakening among the people of the Pacific missions in genealogical and temple work. We believe there is a great future for that work.

Very sincerely your brother,
/signed/William M. Waddoups

# Her Faith Hath Made Her Whole

*Under date of July 7, 1954, Elder Mark E. Petersen of the Council of the Twelve received a letter from a member of the Church in Ogden relating the story of a sister who received a blessing by shaking hands with President McKay. The following is a copy of that letter.*

Dear Brother Petersen:

I feel it a signal honor to have received a letter from you. It is three weeks ago last night at the reception mentioned that I told you of the miraculous happening—yes, blessing—that came to one of our sisters who went to witness the marriage ceremony of my daughter and her fiance.

President McKay, in his masterful manner, performed what was termed an impressive, beautiful rite. Then I being one of the witnesses, and also having been down in Tonga on a mission when President McKay and Brother Hugh J. Cannon toured the mission in 1921-1922, President McKay turned to me and shook my hand, commenting upon being of service to the daughter of a missionary from Tonga and of the pleasant memories of experiences we enjoyed there together. That was the beginning of his shaking hands with twenty-nine or thirty other good people there, a very large wedding group. . . .

My wife is a counselor in the Relief Society of our ward, and Sister Nina Penrod is the other counselor. As President McKay shook Sister Penrod's hand, she asked him if he remembered her mother, a Sister Graham from Ogden Valley. He answered, "Why, of course I do," and placed his left hand on top of her hand as he clasped it in his right. At the moment of the handshake I saw Sister Penrod's face flush. She said she became overwhelmed and humble, more because as both of President's McKay's hands were on her right hand, she felt a shock, and she wondered if others might have heard the sound that accompanied the shock which had seemed very loud to her. She said a weakness came over her. And this is odd, for as President McKay held her right hand with his left hand, he shook hands with many others with his right hand. Sister Penrod said it was very humbling in the extreme to her, yet she felt elated because something wonderful had happened to her, for her arthritis pains were all gone.

We did not see all this, as sixteen of us left for a dinner at the Hotel Utah.

When President McKay left, as it was told to me, Sister Penrod tried to leave with the others but had to be assisted as she was too weak to go alone. They proceeded slowly, and in descending the stairs she cried out, sinking down. She was helped to a bed in the dressing room where after a short time her strength returned and she stood up, turned her back to those with her, and reached each arm up her back, touching her shoulder blades and saying, "I haven't been able to do this for years."

Sister Penrod says she wonders if President McKay knew or was aware that virtue had left him just as the Savior said it had when the woman touched his garment. The incident as related in the Bible seems such a parallel, yet they were dissimilar as they happened. Sister Penrod says she knows faith has made her whole and that God is good. . . .

This experience took place in the new sealing room just to the north of the east temple doors inside the Salt Lake Temple. That was also the first time any of us who were there had seen those doors open when President McKay came in there to officiate on that date—June 15, 1954; time about 1 P.M. This incident is held as a treasured memory.

Yours sincerely,
/signed/Reuben L. Hansen

# A Uruguayan Woman's Faith

*While touring the South American missions during the months of November and December, 1954, and January 1955, Elder Mark E. Petersen of the Council of the Twelve visited Uruguay. While at Montevideo, the headquarters of the Uruguayan Mission, he learned of a miraculous healing. Under date of January 31, 1955, Elder Petersen wrote the following account of that healing.*

At the close of the morning general session in the new meetinghouse at Montevideo on Sunday, December 12, 1954, I was approached by a middle-aged Italian woman by the name of Sister Beathgen. After shaking hands with me and exchanging some pleasantries, she showed me her right hand and asked if I could see the small scar just about an inch below the first finger in the palm of her hand. I told her that I could see it. Then she told me this story:

More than a year ago she was suffering with bone cancer in that hand. A swelling had developed there which made a lump nearly as big as a golf ball. She went to several of the principal doctors of the city and also to the clinics and hospitals of the city, seeking every type of relief. All of the doctors diagnosed it as cancer of the bone. There was no question about the diagnosis as the doctors agreed with each other. The examinations and charts from hospitals indicated the same thing, so she told me. May I say that all of this was confirmed by the mission president and other missionaries who knew this sister during the past couple of years. They also tell me that this is a woman of good reputation, honest and firm and true.

The doctors told her that there was no cure for this cancerous condition. The only thing would be amputation of the arm. She did not wish to have an operation of that kind. When she heard that

President McKay was coming, the thought occurred to her that if she could just shake hands with him her hand would be healed.

With this in mind she stood in line when President McKay was shaking hands with the people following the meetings he attended there in Montevideo. When it came her turn to shake hands, she merely did so and expressed her pleasure at his coming to the conference. She said nothing about her sore hand and said nothing about her hope that she would be healed by shaking the President's hand. She merely shook hands, expressed a few pleasantries, and went on her way.

She told me there in Montevideo that within three days the cancer was gone from her hand. She said further that there had been no recurrence in the past year. I examined her hand again, and it was perfectly free from any kind of sores but merely had a well-healed scar in the palm as I have described.

I talked about this whole situation with the missionaries and President Shreeve, and they confirm this entire story and say that not only do they know that the diagnosis was true but that they themselves also saw this large lump on her hand and knew of this affliction for a fact. They also knew that immediately after the visit of President McKay, Sister Beathgen showed them her hand which was healed.

# "The Eyes of the Blind"

*Brother Melvin T. Mickelson, former superintendent of the Bannock Stake Sunday School, Grace, Idaho, tells his story of regaining his eyesight following administration by President McKay.*

If I were to labor in the service of our Master all the days of my life, I could only repay in part the blessings he has so freely given to me, by the faith and humility of our great leader, President David O. McKay. He, through the power of the priesthood, made it possible for me to enjoy the blessing of sight.

In the month of March 1939, while trucking grain to Salt Lake City from Gem Valley, Idaho, and returning loaded with coal, I was aware of quite a severe headache, but kept on going even though I realized the trouble was in my eyes, particularly my right eye. As this pain increased, I became sick and was getting ready to go to a doctor when I received word that my uncle, Theodore Mickelson, living in Tetonia, Idaho, had passed away and that the family desired that I speak at his funeral. This seemed an opportunity to speak for one whom I loved very much.

I thought perhaps I could see a doctor in Idaho Falls, Idaho. I went to a doctor there, and when he looked at my eyes, he said that my trouble was more than he would like to take care of. He then recommended another doctor in another town whom I went to see. This doctor seemed quite excited about my condition, and he, being a specialist, treated my eyes. At this time I was unable to see anything out of my right eye, and the pain was increasing by the hour. However, I stayed and spoke at the funeral of my uncle.

As soon as I finished speaking, I was brought home by my brother-in-law, Vernon H. Mendenhall. I went immediately to see a doctor at Soda Springs, Idaho, who exclaimed, the minute he examined my eyes, that I was blind. He suggested that I go at once to Salt Lake City, Utah. We arrived there about five o'clock the next morning.

My wife, Mary, called an eye physician, who came to his office about six A.M. After she told him what was wrong he examined my eyes, and then he exclaimed, "Mary, you are a week or ten days too late in coming for aid to save your husband's eye. We may have to remove both of them." I was suffering with iritis. After talking with Mary and me, he decided to fight the infection with medicine.

The doctor worked hard and was very kind, as the treatments were severe and painful. I realized that if I had gone to the doctor as my wife had suggested when I first took sick, most of the trouble could have been stopped.

The doctor advised me to keep on my feet and walk around if possible. This was accomplished only by my wife leading me, for the sight in one eye was completely gone, and the other had sympathized to a point I could not see to get around. For one week the doctor treated my eyes, only to say each day that they were getting worse.

Then one morning the doctor told me he would have to remove my right eye. By so doing the other eye might be saved. About two hours after we had left the doctor's office, President McKay came to our door and told us he had heard of my sickness and wondered if I would like a blessing. No one could deny the feeling of peace which came with him. As he blessed me, the pain eased and then left me. As President McKay left the room, my wife's words of faith were, "You will be all right.". . .

The next morning I returned to the doctor's office. After examining my eyes, he said, "Some miracle has happened. We won't have to remove that eye. Why, you will receive fifteen to twenty percent of your eyesight." The next day he told me that seventy-five percent of my vision would come back, and on the third day, perhaps all of my vision.

I was so humble and thankful that I could not tell the doctor what had happened. I do not know if he knows what happened and why he did not have to perform an operation, but I know.

I am so thankful for our wonderful prophet and his great love and faith and that he took time for one of his fellowmen.

*In a letter dated March 8, 1954, addressed to General Superintendent George R. Hill of the Sunday School, Brother Mickelson stated:*

I don't know why the Lord saw fit to give me such a great blessing when I was so sick, but this I know, that when President McKay was told they were going to remove one of my eyes the next morning, he promised me by the authority which he held that I should be made well and receive my normal vision. No one could possibly know the feeling of joy and peace which came to my wife and me in those few moments we spent with the prophet of God that day; and while his hands were still upon my head the pain, which was greater than I could explain, left my head.

Two or three years later, an eye specialist looked at my eyes and said, "You have a lot of scar-tissue in your eyes, but I have never seen more perfect vision."

I have a desire to serve the Lord in all things and to work wherever I am called, for all that I have I owe to him. With this desire in mind constantly I will help where I am called to serve.

# A Great Healer

*Editorial from the* Deseret News, *September 3, 1954*

To heal the sick in spirit, the depressed in outlook, and the discouraged in hopelessness as well as alleviate the pain and suffering of those desperately ill physically is among the noblest of services. No greater service to his fellows can be rendered by any man than that of raising up by inspiration and divine power those who are spiritually or physically ill and afflicted.

And thus it is fitting that President David O. McKay should be honored next Friday evening with an honorary membership in the International College of Surgeons. The award will be made as a part of the ceremonies of their 19th annual Congress being held in Chicago.

Certainly no layman is more deserving of such an award than is President McKay. On five continents and on the islands of the sea, there are those who can testify not only to his healing power of spirit and faith in their behalf, but also of his successes in their physical healings as well. He has been, on countless occasions, the instrumentality in the Lord's hands of raising from their beds of affliction those who were seriously ill.

This recognition by a distinguished society of scientists and physicians and surgeons of divine healing power, which has been so frequently demonstrated through the administrations of President McKay, is, indeed, a compliment to the College of Surgeons itself. To both of them every Christian believer extends his congratulations!

# When Death Has Called

*From an address by President McKay at the dedicatory services of the San Joaquin Stake Center in California, November 6, 1955.*

We think we live here on earth; we are alive physically, and when death comes, that is the end of our physical existence. But we do not stop to think that probably dying here is living. We die to live. Let me illustrate.

I was called one day to administer to a young man in the Thomas D. Dee Memorial Hospital in Ogden, Utah, a youth named Stewart Eccles. He was irrational, wanted to get out of bed, wanted to get back to his work in Oregon. After the administration he became calm, and I remember his saying, "That's wonderful; that's wonderful."

About a week later I was on a train traveling between Salt Lake City and Ogden, sitting beside this young man's uncle, David Eccles, a multimillionaire. As we got off the train in Ogden, he said, "David, let's go over to the Opera House." "No," I said, "I think I had better go home." "Oh, come, we can sit in a box" (he owned the theater). We had been in the box at the theater but a few minutes when a messenger came in and said, "Uncle David, Stewart is worse. He is at the hospital." We both had thought he was better. We went immediately to the hospital and entered the room where the young man lay unconscious. On the opposite side of the room from where I stood was his mother, weeping. At the foot of his bed was Bertha Eccles Wright, his cousin. His uncle, David, stood by me.

While we stood there, the sick young man spoke as audibly as I am speaking to you: "Yes, Father, I recognize you. May I come back?"

Bertha said, "Oh, Brother McKay, administer to him."

I said, "It is too late, he has gone," and yet he was speaking, and his vocal cords responded. However, in a few moments his heartbeat stopped, and he was gone.

Stewart's father had been dead for some twelve years. No mention had been made of him by those around the bedside. No sound had been made, so far as I knew—not while we stood around there—that would call forth such a response, and yet he spoke those words.

I thought, and I think now, that that young man responded to an environment to which we in our mortal stage were unresponsive. I cannot prove it except that I have witnessed that scene repeated on other instances, including the time when our own little boy passed away.

# Section V

---

# Inspirational
# Stories
# For Youth

# Leading the Youth

By Clare Middlemiss

At one time President McKay said, "Leading youth, leading children to know God, to have faith in his laws, to have confidence in his Fatherhood, and to find solace and peace in his love—this is the greatest privilege, the most sublime opportunity offered the true educator."

For over half a century boys and girls and older ones, too, throughout the Church were touched and impressed by President McKay's stories and illustrations. They were inspired by his great personality, and were led to cherish worthy ideals and noble aspirations. Through his teachings, they came to a realization that there can be no happiness without spirituality, and that the Church is "established as a means of consummating God's purposes."

The following illustrations are a few that were frequently used by this master teacher in leading children, men, and women to know God and the abundant life.

# The Importance of Guiding Youth

*Address delivered at a leadership convention held at Brigham Young University, February 3, 1946.*

Recently I had great pleasure in training a well-bred colt. He had a good disposition, clean, well-rounded eye, was well-proportioned, and all in all, a choice equine possession. Under the saddle he was as willing, responsive, and co-operative as a horse could be. He and my dog "Scotty" were real companions. I liked the way he would go up to something of which he was afraid. He had confidence that if he would do as I bade him he would not be injured.

But "U-Dandy" resented restraint. He was ill-contented when

tied and would nibble at the tie-rope until he was free. He would not run away, just wanted to be free. Thinking other horses felt the same, he would proceed to untie their ropes. He hated to be confined in the pasture, and if he could find a place in the fence where there was only smooth wire, he would paw the wire carefully with his feet until he could step over to freedom. More than once my neighbors were kind enough to put him back in the field. He learned even to push open the gate. Though his depredations were provoking and sometimes expensive, I admired his intelligence and ingenuity.

But his curiosity and desire to explore the neighborhood led him and me into trouble. Once on the highway he was hit by an automobile, resulting in a demolished machine, injury to the horse, and slight, though not serious, injury to the driver.

Recovering from that, and still impelled with a feeling of wanderlust, he inspected the fence throughout the entire boundary. He even found the gates wired. So, for awhile we thought we had "U-Dandy" secure in the pasture.

One day, however, somebody left the gate unwired. Detecting this, "U-Dandy" unlatched it, took "Nig," his companion, with him, and together they visited the neighbor's field. They went to an old house used for storage. "U-Dandy's" curiosity prompted him to push open the door. Just as he had surmised, there was a sack of grain. What a find! Yes, and what a tragedy! The grain was poison bait for rodents! In a few minutes "U-Dandy" and "Nig" were in spasmodic pain, and shortly both were dead.

How like "U-Dandy" are many of our youth! They are not bad; they do not even intend to do wrong, but they are impulsive, full of life, full of curiosity, and long to do something. They, too, are restive under restraint, but if they are kept busy and guided carefully and rightly, they prove to be responsive and capable. However, if they are left to wander unguided, they all too frequently find themselves in the environment of temptation and too often are entangled in the snares of evil.

President David O. McKay astride "U-Sonny Boy," a favorite mount, at his farm in Huntsville, Utah, August 21, 1954.

# "Whate'er Thou Art, Act Well Thy Part"

*From dedicatory address at Sauniatu, Upolu, Samoa, January 15, 1955.*

I remember as a missionary in Scotland fifty-seven years ago, after having been in Stirling only a few weeks, I walked around Stirling Castle with my senior companion, Elder Peter G. Johnston of Idaho. We had not yet secured our lodging in Stirling. I confess I was homesick. I did not like the attitude of the people there, for they were suspicious that we were there for ulterior motives. We had spent half a day around the castle, and the men out in the fields ploughing, that spring day, made me all the more homesick and took me back to my old home town.

As we returned to the town, I saw an unfinished building standing back from the sidewalk several yards. Over the front door was a stone arch, something unusual in a residence, and what was still more unusual, I could see from the sidewalk that there was an inscription chiseled in that arch.

I said to my companion, "That's unusual! I am going to see what the inscription is." When I approached near enough, this message came to me, not only in stone, but as if it came from One in whose service we were engaged: "Whate'er Thou Art, Act Well Thy Part."

I turned and walked thoughtfully away, and when I reached my companion I repeated the message to him.

That was a message to me that morning to act my part well as a missionary of The Church of Jesus Christ of Latter-day Saints. It is merely another way of saying—what is more precious because it comes from the words of the Savior—"Not every one that saith unto me, Lord, Lord, shall enter into the kingdom of heaven, but he that doeth the will of my Father which is in heaven." (Matt. 7:21.)

# Losing Self
# for Others

*Address at the dedication of the Nurses' Residence of the Latter-day Saint Hospital
School of Nursing, Salt Lake City, May 8, 1953.*

True happiness is found in the paradoxical saying of the Savior,
"He that loseth his life for my sake shall find it." (Matt. 10:39.) Our
lives are wrapped up with the lives of others, and we are happiest as
we contribute to their happiness.

This principle is portrayed by Robert Browning in his immortal story of Paracelsus, who selfishly sought fame and glory by
withdrawing from direct contact with his fellowmen. Old age over-
took him before he realized his mistake and before he learned the
great lesson of life. When his friend Festus found him, after a
separation of many years, Paracelsus, lying on a bed in a Greek con-
jurer's house, said, "I am happy; my foot is on the threshold of
boundless life. I see the whole world and hurricane of life behind
me. All my life passes by and I know its purpose, and to what end it
has brought me, and whither I am going. I will tell you all the
meaning of life."

Festus exclaimed, "My friend, tell it to the world!"

Paracelsus: "There was a time when I was happy; the secret of
life was in that happiness."

Festus: "When, when was that? All I hope that answer will
decide."

Paracelsus: "When, but the time I vowed myself to man."

Festus: "Great God, thy judgments are inscrutable."

Paracelsus: "There is an answer to the passionate longings of
the heart for fullness, and I knew it, and the answer is this: Live in
all things outside yourself by love, and you will have joy. That is the
life of God; it ought to be our life. In him it is accomplished and
perfect; but in all created things it is a lesson learned slowly and
through difficulty."

"Serve ye one another by love," writes the apostle; and Jesus
sums it up as follows:

". . . love the Lord thy God with all thy heart, and with all thy soul, and with all thy mind.

"This is the first and great commandment.

"And the second is like unto it, Thou shalt love thy neighbour as thyself.

"On these two commandments hang all the law and the prophets." (Matt. 22:37-40.)

There are those who declare such an ideal merely theoretical; they call it impractical. Why not try it? A test by application will prove its practicability. Let the nations of the world that are today descending the hills of progress and slipping down into the slums and gutters of animal indulgence sneer at the ideals if they will; but as sure as God has given us the revelation of life, so shall we find happiness supreme as we climb the hill of service.

# A Glass of Water and a Drop of Ink

*An illustration and a story on chastity as given by President McKay at a meeting held in the South African Mission, Johannesburg, South Africa, January 10, 1954.*

I am going to tell you a true story, but before I tell you that story I am going to ask some questions, because I never tell a story to children who do not think. There is no use talking to children who do not think. Some teachers make that mistake—they give the lesson, but they do not stop to see whether or not the thoughts are in the minds of the children. If you children will answer a few questions so that I shall know that you are thinking, I will tell a story illustrative of the value of character.

What am I holding in my hand? (President McKay is exhibiting a glass of water.)

"A glass of water."

What kind of water?

"Pure water."

What is this I hold in my hand? (Exhibiting a fountain pen.) (As hands are raised:) Look at those thinkers!

Answer: "A pen."

A pen is right. And what do you think is in that pen? You tell me, young man.

Answer: "Ink."

I am going to take that glass of pure water and put just one drop of ink in it—I think I shall put not even a drop in it, but I shall bring this pen, with ink in it, in contact with that pure water. Now watch. (President McKay inserts the pen and moves it about a bit, and the ink spreads from the pen into the water.) Now what kind of water is in the glass?

Answer: "Impure water."

Yes, I have polluted that water. Should you like to drink it now?

Answer: "No."

No, for I have put ink in that water and made it impure. How many of you have a little baby boy or girl at home? (Hands are raised.) I see. Do you know that that little baby is just as pure and sweet as that pure water I had in the glass; and that it has just come from the presence of our Heavenly Father? One man, as he looked at a baby dressed in white, said:

> *Daisies adorn the fresh meadow,*
> *Lilies gladden the field;*
> *Roses make bright every wayside,*
> *Each twig has some beauty to yield—*
> *All are expressions of Goodness,*
> *And praises to God invite;*
> *But the glory of all creation,*
> *Is a baby dressed in white.*
>
> (From "A Baby Dressed in White,"
> by President David O. McKay.)

Now, imagine that sweet little baby before you this morning, just as that glass of water—and here, again, I want thinkers before I tell you a story.

Will you tell me what might enter that baby's life if you would pollute it, just as that ink polluted the water?

Answer: "Death."

No, death is not such a terrible thing as we think it is. I want to know, while that little baby is in life here, what might go into his soul that could pollute it as that ink did the water.

Answer: "Evil."

Evil is right. Now, will you specify some things which are evil.

Answer: "Sin."

Yes, sin and evil, but I want to know some specific things. As the little baby grows to be your size, a little boy or girl, what might happen that would pollute that child's soul?

Answer: "Disbelief in God."

Thank you. I think that is a very good answer. Now, another thing.

Answer: "Smoking."

Smoking is right! I think it is one of the great evils of our time; just as sure as that ink polluted the water, so will smoking pollute the lives of our boys and girls. Another.

Answer: "Robbing."

Yes, robbing or stealing. The other day a little boy I know stole something and then denied it to his mother. He thought he could hide it. He did not know that there were two people in the world who would know about it whether his mother or anybody else knew it. He himself knew it, *and God knew it*. You never can hide it. Stealing will pollute that little boy's life. (Hands are raised again.) You tell me.

Answer: "Coffee."

That is right. Another.

Answer: "Drinking."

Drinking beer or whiskey, that is right. Another?

Answer: "Taking another's life."

Yes. Infringing in any way. Thank you. Those are the things which pollute. (More hands are raised.)

Answer: "Lying."

Lying! Just as injurious as adding ink to that pure water! And one evil that covers all of them—who can think of one word? Disobedience! Disobeying Mother; disobeying Father; disobeying our Heavenly Father's teachings. Thank you.

\* \* \*

And now, as promised, I will tell you a true story of a young boy who went with his father, an American admiral in the early American history, down to New Orleans in the southern part of the United States to quell a treasonable uprising of Aaron Burr. The admiral's son, David, about twelve years of age, went as his cabin boy.

An admiral controls several ships, as you know, and David was the cabin boy of the admiral of the fleet. He was proud of his position and thought that he was bigger than he was.

Unwisely David took up smoking and swearing. His father worried. He was not a religious man, but he knew that those things would pollute that boy's life, especially while he was young. He therefore cautioned the sailors not to take David into their card games and gambling, or to take him to the bar and treat him with grog. David was learning to like the grog and learning also to like tobacco and swearing, and his father did not like that. He was a bright, active boy, and the sailors liked to have him in the game.

Before they reached New Orleans the father decided there was only one thing to do and that was to get David to decide for himself.

One day after the noon meal, the father dismissed the officers but said to David, "Wait a minute!" After the officers passed to their various duties, the father shut the door and, coming back to David, said, "David, what do you intend to be when you grow up to be a man?"

David threw back his shoulders. "I intend to follow the sea!"

"Yes," said the father, "follow the sea. Be a poor, miserable, drunken sailor, kicked and cuffed about before the mast, and die of fever in some foreign hospital."

"No," said David, "I intend to tread the quarter-deck and command as you do."

The father said, "No, David, no boy ever trod the quarter-deck with such principles as you have, and such habits as you are exhibiting. You will have to change your whole course of life if you grow to be a man."

The father walked out and left David alone.

And like the prodigal son who ate husks with the swine, David came to himself. And he said to himself, "So that is my life, is it—to be a poor, miserable sailor kicked and cuffed about before the mast, and die of fever in some foreign hospital? I'll change my life, and I'll change it now! I'll never drink another drop of intoxicating liquor—I'll never take the name of God in vain again—I'll never gamble!" And he walked out of the door.

In about an hour, three sailors saw David pass, and said, "Come here, and have a game of cards."

"No, thank you," said David.

One said, "What's eating the lad?"

David went on, and then passed some who were drinking, who called out to him, "Come have a drink, Dave."

"No, thank you, I am not taking it anymore."

A few said, "Stay with it, lad."

And David did.

The father quelled the treason of Aaron Burr. That is a matter of United States history, and then he returned.

Years afterward a banquet was given in a leading hotel in New York City in honor of an admiral who had won distinction in a recent war. He was the honored guest, and when the chairman arose to introduce him, he introduced Admiral David Farragut of the United States Navy, who, when he arose to acknowledge the welcome, said, "Should you men like to know to what I owe my success in the Navy?" and a round of applause was the answer. And this is what he said: "It was all owing to a resolution I formed when I was a young boy, twelve years of age, acting as cabin boy to my father, who went to New Orleans to quell the treason of Aaron Burr."

And then he repeated in detail what I have given you in a general way only—the conversation between the father and himself. When he came to that part where he made the resolution never to drink another drop of intoxicating liquor and never to take the name of God in vain, he added: "As God is my witness, I have kept that vow to this day."

*The illustration of a drop of ink made a lasting impression on a young boy forty years ago, and when Marion G. Romney was sustained as a member of the Council of the Twelve in a general conference meeting held in the Salt Lake Tabernacle on October 4, 1951, he paid the following tribute to President McKay.*

I have loved President McKay for a long, long time. He doesn't remember when I first fell in love with him. I guess he doesn't remember when you did either.

It was down in Los Angeles in the winter of 1912 and 1913. We were known then as Mormon refugees. We had lost our homes in Mexico—invited out down there. Brother McKay came to Los Angeles; he came to Sunday School, and he took a glass of water. He had a pen in his hand. He showed us how clear and beautiful the water was, and then he dropped a drop of ink in the water, and it clouded it all through, and he said to us little fellows, "That is what sin does to a life," and I have ever since then, President McKay, been trying to keep that sin out of my life.

# The Story of Fua

*Incident of 1921 world tour of missions as related September 9, 1940.*

In midsummer of 1921, Hugh J. Cannon, several elders, and I were quarantined on the island of Makaka'a, Tonga. On that small island twenty-nine people had to remain for two weeks before the Tongan government would permit them to land at Nukualofa.

One of the government attendants of this group was a Latter-day Saint Tongan youth about nineteen or twenty years of age, named Fua. Fua had never before sought the job of waiter, and he chose it this time merely to make sure that the visiting missionaries would receive proper attention. He feared that because of general prejudice they might be neglected, slighted, or inconvenienced. The young man proved to be an excellent attendant, not only to the elders but also to all whom he served.

When, after two weeks, the quarantine was raised, a government official said to Fua, "Your work has been so satisfactory, we should like to employ you for the next company."

"Thank you," said Fua, "but I am going to visit the islands with the elders."

"We will pay you more than they will pay you," said the government official.

"They pay me nothing," answered Fua.

"What!" exclaimed the official. "Do you mean to say you will give up this job at twice your present wages and go with those men for nothing?"

"Yes," said Fua, "I shall do it gladly."

And he did.

Membership in the Church and instruction in gospel truths in the organization of the Church and the companionship of leading Church officials meant more to Fua than dollars and cents. To a true Latter-day Saint, the gospel is the "pearl of great price," and a heartfelt appreciation of the Church brings a joy and peace of soul that cannot be found in worldly acquisitions alone.

*When President David O. McKay returned to Tonga, he was a speaker at a general meeting held at the Liahona College, Tongatapu, January 11, 1955. He told the audience of some of his memories of thirty-four years ago. He recalled some of his very dear friends whom he met in Tonga at that time. He learned that very morning that one of them had died two years ago. He was young Fua regarding whom the above incident is related. The President deeply regretted that he did not have the opportunity once again to see Fua, whose story of faith and loyalty he told on countless occasions. President McKay then told this story of another Tongan, a young man who joined the Church.*

This young man's parents and some of the government officials tried to get him to renounce his religion, and they offered him an enticing amount of money if he would give it up. . . . However, that young man said, "Do you see those islands? Well, if you owned all of them and offered them to me if I would give up my religion, I should refuse your offer because I know that this religion is true."

I remember with gratitude that expression of faith and loyalty. Many of those young men then, and others who remember me when I was on that memorable visit in 1921, I have been happy to meet today.

# Business Executive in Prayer

*From an address delivered at Ricks College commencement exercises, Rexburg, Idaho, May 24, 1954.*

Start your day each morning by expressing to God gratitude for this glorious old world, for your life in it, for your citizenship in this great republic, for the liberty vouchsafed by the Constitution. Invoke his guidance and help in whatever you undertake to do.

There is a story of a manager of one of the largest manufacturing plants in the United States who was known as a rather reserved, quiet, but most efficient executive. One day a factory superintendent sought the manager in his office and was told by the secretary, who sat in an outer office, that the manager was "in conference" and was "not to be disturbed."

"But how can he be in conference? There's nobody in the office but himself," expostulated the superintendent, an impetuous sort of man. He had seen the manager enter the office alone. "I must see him on a matter of great importance," and he pushed by the secretary, even after she said, "You may come back in a few moments, but at present he is not to be disturbed."

The superintendent pushed by the secretary, as I say, and quickly opened the door to the manager's private office. Then after a quick glance within, he quietly closed the door and turned and faced the secretary, "Why, he is on his knees!"

"Yes, in conference, as I told you," said the secretary.

"I—I'm sorry. I didn't know he was that sort of man," apologized the superintendent. "I guess there was One in there with him of greater importance than I." And he went away, still with an amazed look on his face.

# Moral Courage

*From an address delivered at Liberty Stake Theme Festival May 6, 1941.*

It takes moral courage to maintain ideals. Moral courage springs from sincerity, the unassuming, most substantial virtue of the human soul. Everyone experiences a thrill at a feat involving physical courage, but the greatest heroes have won their laurels in manifestations of moral courage. Take, for example, John the Baptist denouncing the sensual Herod, Peter before the Sanhedrin, Paul in a Roman dungeon, Luther at the Diet of Worms, Joseph Smith facing Carthage and martyrdom, and Christ before Pilate and on the cross.

The story is told of a boy who was a total abstainer and who was about to be apprenticed to a trade. The foreman of the place offered him a glass of beer, but the lad refused, saying he never drank such stuff. Somewhat irritated, the foreman said angrily, "We have no teetotalers in this place."

"You'll have one if you have me," said the lad.

More irritated than ever, the foreman cried, "Look here, boy, you must have this beer inside or outside."

"Well," answered the little fellow, "you can please yourself, sir. I came here this morning with a clean jacket and a clean character. You can soil my jacket if you like, but you cannot spoil my character."

That's moral courage. Let me tell you young men and young women that the world expects that from you and from me. Don't you ever believe that you can gain favor by yielding; you lose favor by doing so.

# Temporal Salvation of Man

*Taken from an address at a Church welfare meeting in the Salt Lake Tabernacle, April 5, 1941.*

In 1897 when I was on my first mission, I found myself distributing tracts one morning, in a little undesirable district in Stirling, Scotland. I approached one door and in answer to the knock a haggard woman stood before me, poorly dressed, with sunken cheeks and unkempt hair. As she received the tract I offered, she said, in a rather harsh voice, "Will this buy me any bread?" As I started to tell her that it would buy her not only bread but something far more precious, a man equally haggard and underfed came up and said; "What is it?" She handed the tract to the man and said, "Gospel vendor! Shut the door!" From that moment I had a deeper realization that the church of Christ should be and is interested in the temporal salvation of man. I walked away from the door feeling that that couple, with the bitterness in their hearts toward man and God, were in no position to receive the message of the gospel. They were in need of temporal help, and there was no organization, so far as I could learn, in Stirling that could give it to them.

# Dad Held the Rope

*From an address delivered at the annual convention of the Primary Association in the Assembly Hall, June 9, 1934.*

A party of English botanists last summer spent their vacation in the Swiss Alps collecting specimens of rare flowers. They started out one morning from a small village and after a several hours' climb came to a precipice overlooking a green valley dotted with a peculiar flower, which, examined through field glasses, proved to be of unusual value. From the cliff on which the party was standing to the valley was a sheer drop of several hundred feet. To descend would be impossible, and to reach the valley from another approach would mean a waste of several hours.

During the latter part of their climb a small boy had attached himself to the party and had watched with interest the maneuvers of the botanists. After discussing the situation for several minutes, one of the party turned to the boy and said, "Young fellow, if you will let us tie a rope around your waist and lower you over this cliff so that you can dig up one of those plants for us, and let us pull you back up, without harming the plant, we will give you five pounds."

The boy looked dazed for an instant, then ran off, apparently frightened at the prospect of being lowered over the cliff by a rope. Within a short time he returned, bringing with him an old man, bent and gray, with hands gnarled and calloused by hard labor. Upon reaching the party of botanists the boy turned to the man who had made the offer and said, "Sir, this is my dad. I'll go down in the valley if you'll let my dad hold the rope!"

It is possible for a teacher to win just such trust from his pupils, to shatter which is short of criminal. Interest and confidence are gained only by example, not by precept.

# A Gentleman's Word of Honor

*From an address delivered to executives of the National Council of the Boy Scouts of America, held in the Statler Hotel, Los Angeles, California, July 17, 1953.*

Great men esteem their word of honor above their signed note.

This is illustrated by an English gentleman who found himself distressed financially, and borrowed from a friend, to whom he gave his written note, properly signed. Before the gentleman's income was sufficient to repay that note, he had found it necessary to borrow from another friend, to whom he gave only his promise. Both of these lenders learned when the gentleman received his income, and both called for the return of their money. The borrower was about to pay the second lender first; and the first protested, saying: "Your honor, I lent you the money first, and should receive payment."

"Yes," said the English gentleman, "that is true, but you have my signed note. This gentleman has only my word of honor. I wish to redeem my word of honor first."

The friend who had given the first loan took from his pocket the signed note and tore it into shreds before the borrower. "There," said the lender, "now I have only your word of honor."

"In that case," said the gentleman, "I will pay you first."

# Dangerous Reefs

*From a general conference address April 8, 1945.*

Twenty-four years ago when the steamship *Marama* dropped anchor outside the coral reef that surrounds the island of Rarotonga, a passenger desiring to go ashore asked the captain why he did not sail nearer the wharf. In answer the experienced seaman mentioned treacherous waters and pointed to an engine of one ship, the *Maitai*, and to the bow of another, still protruding out of the water—both carrying mute evidence of the danger of anchoring too close to the shore of this coral-bound island. "We anchor here," said the captain, "because it is safer to avoid being dashed to pieces, as were those two vessels, hulls of which lie on those dangerous reefs."

A flippant attitude toward marriage, the ill-advised suggestion of "companionate marriage," the base, diabolical theory of "free sex experiment," and the ready-made divorce courts are dangerous reefs upon which many a family bark is wrecked.

# The Rapids Are Below

*From a general conference address delivered October 8, 1920.*

I am reminded of an old story that appeared in one of our early schoolbooks. Many of you will remember it. You will recall that the author pictures some people sailing down the river toward Niagara Falls, and the man on the shore cries, "Young men, ahoy, the rapids are below you!" But they went on laughing and carousing. Later he cried, "Young men, ahoy, the rapids are below you!"

But they heeded not his warning call until they suddenly realized that they were in the midst of the rapids, but with all the power at their command they failed to turn their boat upstream—so shrieking and cursing over they went!

Well, it is a very impressive picture. The lesson left an indelible impression upon me, but now it seems incomplete. It is one thing to stand on the shore and cry, "Young men, ahoy, there is danger ahead." It is another thing to row into the stream and, if possible, get into the boat with the young men and, by companionship, by persuasion, by legitimate force, when necessary, turn the boat from the rapids. Too many of us stand on the shore and cry, "Young men, ahoy!" Let us get into their lives, let us touch their personality by our personality, and let them feel that there is something real in this religion—that it is the greatest thing in life, that nothing else can make them live as the true religious life.

# The Nettles

*From address to Parent-Teachers Association of Ensign School, Salt Lake City, November 14, 1935.*

Jean Valjean as Monsieur l'Mayor—you will remember, in that great work of Victor Hugo's *Les Miserables*—came one day upon some laborers who were very busy pulling up the nettles. The nettles were lying there—thrown out to die. The great leader picked up one and said, "This is dead, but it would be well if we knew how to put it to some use. When the nettle is young, the leaves make excellent greens; even when old it has filaments and fibers like hemp and flax. Cloth made from the nettle is worth as much as that made from hemp. Chopped up, the nettle is good for poultry; pounded, it is good for horned cattle."

He named some other uses and added, "If we would take a little pain, the nettle would be useful; we neglect it, and it becomes harmful, then we kill it."

He then paused and said, "How much men are like nettles! My friends, remember this, that there are no bad herbs and no bad men. There are only bad cultivators!"

I think the man or woman who stands before a class to teach the standards of the Church who himself or herself does not live up to those standards is a "bad cultivator."

# The Rose, the Hawthorn Twig, and the Lily

*From address at an Argentine Mission conference, Buenos Aires, Argentina, February 7, 1954.*

Many years ago Japan was walled in as a nation. During that time learned men studied nature and met little groups of men and women at night and taught them lessons on life.

One morning when one of these learned men was about to leave the gates of the city to go out to study nature, a workman stopped him and said, "When you come in tonight from your studies, will you please bring me a rose, that I may study the whorl of the petals as you pointed out last night?"

"Yes," said the learned man, "I will bring you a rose."

He had not gone far before a second man accosted him, saying,

"Will you please bring me a hawthorn twig tonight?"

"Yes," said the professor.

And even before he got through the gate, a third accosted him, saying, "Will you please bring me a lily that I might see the lessons of purity that you gave us last evening?"

And the professor answered, "I will bring you a lily."

Just as the sun was setting in the west, the professor entered the gate of the city, where the three men met him. To the first he gave the rose; to the second he gave the hawthorn twig; to the third he gave the lily.

Suddenly the man with the rose said, "Why, here's a thorn on the stem of my rose!" And the second said, "And here's a dead leaf clinging to my hawthorn twig!" And the third, encouraged by that faultfinding, said, "And here's dirt clinging to the roots of my lily!"

The professor took the rose from the first, the twig from the second, the lily from the third. He broke the thorn from the stem of the rose and handed it to the first; he plucked the dead leaf from the twig and put it into the hands of the second; he took the dirt from the roots of the lily and gave to the third. Keeping the rose, the twig, and the lily, he said, "There, each of you has what attracted him first. You looked for the thorn and found it. It was there. I left it purposely. The dead leaf was left on the twig, and you saw it first. Purposely I left the dirt on the roots of the lily, and the dirt was the first thing you saw. Each of you keep what attracted your attention; I will keep the rose, the twig, and the lily for the beauty I see in them."

In our branches, in our churches, in our cities, in our nations, we can see in the lives of our fellowmen perhaps a thorn, perhaps a dead leaf, perhaps dirt as in the case of the woman whom the Pharisees thrust at the feet of the Savior. But we shall be happier and better if we see the rose, and the twig, and the lily in the character and the lives of those with whom we associate.

# Maintaining
# the Ideals of the
# Church

*Taken from a letter from President McKay to members of the Church in the Tahitian Mission, dated March 31, 1939.*

When I visited the beautiful island of Tahiti in 1921, I learned of an incident associated with Brother Vaio (a member of the Church), who was then captain of one of the government schooners.

The newly appointed governor of the island was to make a tour of inspection of a government-owned vessel. Captain Vaio and his associates decorated their ship, placed fruits and delicacies on the table, and made ready for a suitable and appropriate reception for His Excellency. A glass of wine was placed at each plate with which at the proper time all would respond to the toast and drink to the health of the governor. There was one exception, however—at Captain Vaio's plate there was placed a glass of lemonade. One of his associates protested, saying that he would offend the governor if he drank only lemonade at the toast, but notwithstanding these protestations Brother Vaio insisted that he would drink only lemonade when the toast was proposed.

It was Captain Vaio's responsibility and honor to make the welcome speech. This he did, and at the conclusion he explained, in substance:

"Your Excellency, before proposing the toast I wish to explain why I am drinking lemonade instead of the customary wine. I am a member of The Church of Jesus Christ of Latter-day Saints. Every Sunday morning I teach a class of young people. It is one of our tenets not to drink wine nor strong drink, tea nor coffee, nor use tobacco. I cannot consistently tell them not to use intoxicating liquor and then indulge myself; therefore, you will understand why on this occasion I am drinking lemonade. And now I propose a toast to the health and happiness of His Excellency, governor of Tahiti."

There was a tense silence among the ship's crew as the

governor arose to make his response. He was a true gentleman and appreciated the loyalty and manhood of the man who had given the welcoming speech. In substance the governor said:

"Captain Vaio, I thank you and your associates for this hearty welcome, and I am glad to learn that you maintain the ideals of your church in regard to temperance. I wish we had more men with such sterling character to take charge of the government's ships."

As we sailed that evening toward Rarotonga, I wondered in admiration how many of the members of the Church were as loyal to the ideals and teachings of the gospel as was Captain Vaio; and the words of the Savior came to my mind as they come again as I dictate these lines: "Not every one that saith unto me, Lord, Lord, shall enter into the kingdom of heaven; but he that doeth the will of my Father which is in heaven." (Matt. 7:21.)

I have learned that Captain Vaio has gone to his eternal reward. Perhaps he knows how many times I have told this story to Sunday School children, not a few of whom, let us hope, have been encouraged along the pathway of duty, because of his courage and loyalty to what he knew was right.

# Sacrifice
# Brings Blessings

*From "A Solution for Present-day Problems,"* Millennial Star, *vol. 31, p. 709.*

Just how sacrifice brings us closer to the Lord I think we can better understand if I relate to you the story of a father whose son had been away nearly two years. The financial depression had hit the father. He was an architect. Building had ceased, and the father's income had become quite limited. A letter came from the son that he needed forty-two or forty-four dollars. The father did not have it. He did not know where to get it, but he wanted his son not to be without the necessary funds. Well, what could he do? He could do just what every true Latter-day Saint does—exercise his faith in God.

To that end he and his wife, in evening prayer, prayed that the way might be opened for them to send their son the money asked for. They retired that night as usual. The next morning he went to his work, not knowing any source from which that forty dollars and more could come.

Toward evening a man came in the office and said, "Two years ago or more you did some architectural work for me, and I could not pay you. You told me not to worry about it, to pay you whenever I wanted to. I had forgotten it until last evening. I have come here now to give you my check."

The father, quite overcome, said, "How did you happen to think of this? I had forgotten it entirely."

The man answered, "My wife and I were coming from Lagoon last night. Your name came up in the conversation, and it was she who asked, 'Have you ever paid him that bill?' I answered 'No,' and said, 'I will attend to that tomorrow.' "

The father said, "At what time was that?" and the architect's heart filled with gratitude when he realized that it was just a few minutes after he and his wife had knelt in prayer, asking God to open the way.

Well, you may say it was a coincidence. Others may say it was merely an association of ideas when the name came up, but to that father and mother it was the direct interposition of God, and their faith in him was more implicit than ever before.

# Man...the Jewel of God

*Testimony given by President McKay at the 139th Semiannual General Conference of the Church in the Salt Lake Tabernacle in October 1969.*

The Church urges men to have self-mastery, to control their appetites, their tempers, and their speech. A man is not at his best when he is a slave to some habit. A man is not his best who lives

With characteristic inspiration President David O. McKay is shown challenging a congregation to the better life.

merely to gratify his passions. That is one reason why the Lord has given the Church the revelation of the Word of Wisdom so that, even from boyhood and girlhood, young men and young women may learn to control themselves. That is not always easy. The youth today face enemies—false ideologies and immoral practices "glossed over" and "seasoned with a text." Sound preparation is necessary to meet and conquer these enemies. Keep in mind that man's earthly existence is but a test as to whether he will concentrate his efforts, his mind, and his soul upon things that contribute to the comfort and gratification of his physical nature, or whether he will make as his life's purpose the acquisition of spiritual qualities.

The spiritual road has Christ as its ideal, not the gratification of the physical, for he that will save his life, yielding to the first gratification of a seeming need, will lose his life, lose his happiness, lose the pleasure of living at this present time. If he would seek the real purpose of life, the individual must live for something higher than self. He hears the Savior's voice saying, "I am the way, the truth, and the life. . . ." (John 14:6.)

Following that light, man soon learns that there is no one great thing he can do to attain happiness or eternal life. He learns that "life is made up, not of great sacrifices and duties, but of little things, in which smiles and kindness, and small obligations given habitually, are what win and preserve the heart and secure comfort."

Spirituality, our true aim, is the consciousness of victory over self, and of communion with the Infinite. Spirituality impels one to conquer difficulties and acquire more and more strength. To feel one's faculties unfolding, and truth expanding in the soul, is one of life's sublimest experiences.

The man who sets his heart upon the things of this world, who does not hesitate to cheat his brother, who will lie for gain, who will steal from his neighbor, or who, by slander, will rob another of his reputation, lives on a low animal plane of existence and either stifles his spirituality or permits it to lie dormant. To be thus carnally minded is to be spiritually dead.

We are truly living in an age of changing opinions, of swiftly shifting human relations. Man's wisdom seems baffled. In all our readjustments, plans, and policies we cannot do better than keep in mind the divine admonition that "the worth of souls is great in the sight of God." The saved individual is the supreme end of the divine will.

Jesus sought the welfare of the individual, and individuals grouped and laboring for the general welfare of the whole in conformity with the principles of the gospel constitute the kingdom of God. Many of the choicest truths of the gospel were given in conversations with individuals. It was while Jesus talked with Nicodemus that he gave us the message relative to baptism and being born again. From the conversation with the woman of Samaria is disclosed the truth that they who worship God must worship in spirit and in truth. From that with Mary and Martha, we get the divine declaration: "I am the resurrection, and the life: he that believeth in me, though he were dead, yet shall he live." (John 11:25.) Jesus' regard for personality was supreme. When the Pharisees dragged into his presence the woman taken in adultery, he saw through the soul that had been stained with sin the personality that still contained the spark of hope, which he kindled into a light that warmed and guided a personality back to confidence and perhaps to righteousness.

To members of The Church of Jesus Christ of Latter-day Saints, the worth of the individual has a special meaning. Quorums, auxiliaries, wards, stakes—even the Church itself—are all organized to further the welfare of man. All are but means to an end, and that end is the happiness and eternal welfare of every child of God. I therefore appeal to all members of the Church, and particularly to presidents of quorums and to officers of all auxiliaries, to put forth a unified effort to make sweeter and better the lives of men.

Supplant the thought that dominates the selfish world, as expressed in the words "The world owes me a living," by the nobler prayer, "God, give me power to lend a helping hand to others."

Keep as a guiding principle the consciousness that the ultimate purpose of life is the perfecting of the individual. This implies an intelligence directing creation, and to me it implies a divine personality, a beneficent Father.

I love the young people, and my heart goes out to them. May God keep them true to the faith and bless them that they will be able to withstand the temptations that constantly beset their paths. To the youth of the Church I say, Go to your Father in heaven in prayer; seek the advice of your parents, your bishops, and your stake presidents.

To the members of the Church everywhere I say, Live honest, sincere lives! Be honest with yourselves, honest with your brethren, honest with your families, honest with those with whom you deal— always honest! The very foundation of all character rests upon the principles of honesty and sincerity.

Be true to the Church. Be true to your families—loyal to them. Protect your children and guide them, not arbitrarily but by example.

I bear you my witness that the teachings of our Lord and Savior Jesus Christ contain the true philosophy of living. I make no exception. I love them. There are men who say that they are not applicable to this day, but I say they are as applicable today as they were when he spoke them; and, because they contain eternal truths, they will be applicable through all time.

God help us to understand these eternal truths, and may he give us power to live them.

# A Lover of Animals

In the lovely mountain valley where Huntsville, Utah, was located, David had a happy childhood. He was surrounded by pleasures for which every boy longs. He had his own pets, which he loved—a dog, a pony, many rabbits and pigeons, and a magpie whom he tamed and trained to talk.

One day Bishop McKay returned from Dry Hollow, bringing a wet baby magpie that had fallen from its nest high up in a cottonwood tree. The tiny bird was wrapped in a piece of warm flannel cloth and placed near the stove until it was perfectly dry; then it was fed, and it soon became quite at home with the McKay children. David made a cage out of a crate, tacking wire netting across the front and making a slide door on the side through which food and water could be placed inside.

David named the pet Jock and became very devoted to him. One day a friend suggested, "You will have to split his tongue if you want to teach him to talk." David was shocked and replied, "I wouldn't think of hurting Jock that way if he never learned to talk." But through David's kindness and patience, and much repetition, the bird learned to speak quite plainly and became the wonder of the neighborhood.

One day President McKay related to his secretary this incident about his pet Jock. He said that his mother let him have the magpie cage in the house, and that sometimes she would let him open the cage door and let Jock fly around the room. Then he said, "You know, that magpie used to pick up mother's needle which was threaded; fly around the room and down on the carpet; pick up one end of it, hide the needle and thread under the carpet—and then go back to his cage and laugh!" He said, "I spent a lot of time teaching that magpie to talk. It could say 'Hello, Jock.' But after about a year, it got the homing instinct and flew away with some other magpies that came to the valley. However," he added, "I think later that spring it came back two or three times to see me." President McKay thought that he recognized Jock with some other magpies that flew around when they were feeding the chickens and that he heard him say, "Hello, Jock." He really missed this pet.

As a young boy and throughout his life, President McKay was never able to stand to see anyone cruel to animals. When he was a young apostle, he and Sister McKay and their family lived in Huntsville during the summer months. There he taught his own children to take care of their pets and the other animals on the farm.

The family had a boar that they named Caesar. One time, Elder McKay had an assignment to attend a stake conference out of the state. Just as he was leaving home, Caesar broke out of his pen, and Elder McKay caught him and quickly put him in an empty chicken coop and locked the door. He had meant to tell one of the boys where he had put Caesar, but in his haste to catch his train, he forgot to do this.

Late that night, the ringing of the telephone awakened the whole McKay household. When one of the boys answered the telephone, the following telegram, signed David O. McKay, was read by the Western Union Telegraph clerk: "Caesar's in the chicken coop—water him."

David loved to swim in the old swimming hole in Spring Creek—to ice-skate and sleighride; but most of all he loved to ride his pony, bareback, up into the hills east of Huntsville.

# Going Away to College

*With their father in the driver's seat of their rugged farm wagon, young David Oman McKay; his brother, Thomas E., and their sisters Jeannette and Annie, left Huntsville in the fall of 1894 for Salt Lake City, where they would live while attending the University of Utah. David and Thomas sold the milk from their cow to help defray their school expenses. The following is taken from an article in the* Church News *August 12, 1961.*

A rugged, old farm wagon drawn by a team of horses lumbered out of Huntsville one morning in the fall of 1894 and headed down Ogden Canyon. It was loaded with some boxes and trunks filled with clothing and with a generous supply of flour and bottled fruit and vegetables. A cow from the family herd plodded along behind.

Bishop David McKay was in the driver's seat. Perched on the cargo were four of his children: David Oman, Thomas E., Jeannette, and Annie. The bishop was not wealthy, but he wanted his children to have a good education. He was taking them to Salt Lake City where they would live while they attended the University of Utah.

Young David's ambition was to teach. Already he had served as principal and teacher for a year at the little school in his hometown after completing two years of study at Weber Stake Academy in Ogden. He also had taught in the Huntsville Ward Sunday School.

He was looking forward to the day when he would leave the university and launch into the field of education armed with a full-fledged teacher's certificate.

He was outstanding at the university in his studies and in extracurricular activities. He was elected president of his class and played guard on the school's first football team. David also found time to court lovely Emma Ray Riggs, his landlady's daughter.

At graduation time in 1897, David was chosen valedictorian. He was prepared to accept a teaching position in a Salt Lake County school and had long ago made up his mind that he was going to marry Emma Ray.

A bomb could not have exploded his plans any more abruptly than the mission call which arrived at this crucial time. But there was no question about what should be done. David was soon on his way to the land of his forefathers, the British Isles. While on his mission, he heard President James McMurrin prophesy that he (Elder McKay) would someday "sit in the leading councils of the Church."

When he returned from his mission in 1899, Elder McKay joined the Weber Stake Academy faculty. He also became a member of the Weber Stake Sunday School board.

Emma Ray had waited for him, and they were married in the Salt Lake Temple on January 2, 1901.

# Three Gates of Gold

*From an address delivered in Town Hall, Adelaide, Australia, February 2, 1955.*

One of our duties as members of the Church is not to find fault, not to criticize unjustly. How many hearts are broken because of the misjudgment of our fellowman? There is something in human nature that seems to rejoice at another's downfall.

Emerson, who is reputedly one of the wisest Americans, speaking on that something in human nature which wishes evil of one another, said, "An accident cannot happen in the street, but the bystanders will be animated with the faint hope that the victim may die."

I think another illustration will be more effective. An old woman, with a shawl around her shoulders, was walking along the river bank near Paris. She stooped, picked up some article, and put it under her shawl. A policeman standing at a distance saw her. Instantly he approached her and said, "Give me that which you have hidden in your shawl." Well, that was conforming to his duty, but his thoughts were not complimentary. He misjudged her, for she withdrew from her shawl a broken piece of glass; placing it in his hands, she said, "I picked it up thinking that perhaps some barefoot boy might step on it."

"Judge not, that ye be not judged. For with what judgment ye judge, ye shall be judged: and with what measure ye mete, it shall be measured to you again. And why beholdest thou the mote that is in thy brother's eye, but considerest not the beam that is in thine own eye? . . . first cast out the beam out of thine own eye; and then shalt thou see clearly to cast out the mote out of thy brother's eye." (Matt. 7:1-3, 5.)

We used to sing a beautiful hymn:

> *Nay, speak no ill; a kindly word*
> *Can never leave a sting behind;*
> *And, oh, to breathe each tale we've heard*
> *Is far beneath a noble mind.*
> *Full oft a better seed is sown*
> *By choosing thus the kinder plan,*
> *For, if but little good is known,*
> *Still let us speak the best we can.*

— *Hymns,* no. 116

That reminds me of a story I once read, that whenever we are receiving a tale, it should pass three gates of gold. "If you're tempted to reveal a tale someone to you has told about another, make it pass, before you speak, three gates of gold. Three narrow gates. First, is it true? Then is it needful? [In your mind, give a truthful answer.] And the third is the last and narrowest, is it kind? And if it reach your lips at last, and you let it through these gateways pass, then you may tell the tale, nor fear what result the speech may be."

I know of nothing in our church, in our state, in our nation, in international relationships, that tends to produce more disunity, more unhappiness, and, when applied to international conditions, more hate, than the slander, the falsehoods, the tale bearing, the magnifying of one another's faults.

I ask you to ask in your hearts if that is true. I know that in our church, when one man is released by the president, he may feel offended and find fault with his actions. Perhaps there will be a reason. But for your own sake, do not say anything about it; for the good of the Church, do not say anything about it. That is the president's responsibility; it is not yours. I know you might feel embarrassed about being released; you might feel that it is a reflection upon your intelligence, upon your leadership. All right, you are a bigger and better man if you say nothing about it and go along with the authorities of the Church.

I had a great lesson from my father on that one principle. He had been bishop in the ward for twenty-three years—twenty-three years of willing service in that little Huntsville Ward of eight hundred members. Then he was released, and a young man was appointed bishop. Mother had died. One day I went up to the home. Father was there alone. I said, "Father, come on down to Ogden with me and visit with us." I then gave some reasons why he should come. He said, "No I can't go tonight." I said, "Why?" He said, "Because I have my ward teaching to do." I thought to myself, The new bishop of this ward was blessed by my father when he was a baby. My father ordained him a deacon, saw him grow in the office of the Church. Now that young man is bishop, and my father is accepting an assignment from him. And he did it gladly. No wonder he was later ordained a patriarch and became the president of the high priests quorum in the stake; and when he was called to answer the final summons, those hundreds of high priests walked by the hearse in tribute to a great soul.

"Judge not, that ye be not judged." Speak well of one another.

Let us set an example of harmony and peace to the world. Let us prove that whether we're in Africa, South America, New Zealand, or Australia, we're all one in Christ. We have only one object in view: to declare to the world that the gospel of Jesus Christ is restored in its fulness, and that the gospel of Jesus Christ is the only plan given to man by which the peace of towns, the peace of nations may eventually come.

# Prayers Answered in Shipwreck

*In August 1899 the steamship* City of Rome *collided with an iceberg just off the coast of Newfoundland. There was panic aboard the vessel, and for a time passengers wondered whether they would have to take to the lifeboats. Among the passengers aboard the ship was David O. McKay, who was returning home from his mission to Great Britain. He related some of the experiences of the passengers following the shipwreck, and the following account was recorded by his secretary, Clare Middlemiss.*

He told of the impact when the bow of the ship ploughed into the iceberg just off the coast of Newfoundland, and of the confusion and panic aboard ship that followed. He said that he ran up to the deck of the ship to see what had happened. On the side of the ship he was on, he could stretch out his arm and touch the iceberg, and he was very concerned when he saw the predicament they were in.

Very little progress could be made by the ship during that dreadful night, but the missionaries and Saints who were aboard ship gathered together and prayed for God's help and protection during that critical time. President McKay said that it was a miracle how the captain was able to maneuver the ship through and around that iceberg until they were in the clear and could proceed in safety from the danger that had threatened them.

President McKay told how thankful and grateful they were for the protection of the Lord, and said that he knew that the fervent prayers of the missionaries, the Saints, and himself had been answered. He said he also felt that the Lord's hand had directed the captain in guiding the ship away from the huge iceberg that the bow of the *City of Rome* had struck.

# "Make Me a Boy, Just for Tonight"

*On Friday, October 10, 1958, President McKay dedicated the Aaronic Priesthood Monument on Temple Square in Salt Lake City. These remarks were given in a dedicatory address in the Salt Lake Tabernacle prior to the dedicatory prayer at the monument.*

A poet once wrote:

*Backward, turn backward, O Time in your flight,*

*Make me a boy again, just for tonight.*

These exercises tonight, impressive, inspiring, have done that to me in memory. I remember as a deacon chopping wood for the widows on Saturday. We met as a group of nine boys, held a short meeting, took our axes, went to the widows, and chopped enough wood for each to last that week.

As a teacher in the Aaronic Priesthood, I recall my first ward teaching visit with Eli Tracy. I remember the first house we entered. But predominantly there comes to my mind a story that Eli told me as we walked from one house to another, how he had formed the habit of smoking before he joined the Church. When he made up his mind to stop it, he took his pipe and tobacco, put them on the mantlepiece where he could see them, and said, "Now, you stay there. I am never going to touch you again." And he never did. A man had added dignity to his manhood, strength of character. I never forgot it.

As a priest, I recall administering the sacrament and my failure the first time I offered the prayer. We did not have the prayer on a printed card before us then as is frequently the case now. We were supposed to memorize it. The sacrament table was just under the pulpit, and my father, the bishop, always stood right over the one who asked the blessing upon the bread and water. I thought I knew the prayer, but I had memorized it privately, and when I knelt and saw the congregation before me, I became flustered. I remember when I got to the words "that they are willing to take upon them the name of thy Son." Everything went blank and I said, "Amen." Father said, "And always remember him. . . ." I was half rising from my knees, but I knelt down again and said, "And always remember him. Amen." Father said, ". . . and keep his commandments which he has given them." I knelt down again: ". . . and keep his commandments which he has given them. Amen." ". . . that they may always have his Spirit to be with them. Amen."

I suffered all the pangs of failure, but I am glad that we did not give up.

Yes, the memories of childhood stay with you and contribute to the character that you build. I mention these incidents reminiscently, just merely in passing, to tell you that years soon pass between boyhood, manhood, old age. It does not seem long ago, but life is made up of just such experiences. It is the service that you render and the character that you build that you can take back to your Heavenly Father—the only two things. If you are old enough and have your family, you will have your family, your wife, and your children throughout eternity.

One man has said that all that you can take to have and to hold when death comes is the service that you have rendered mankind. This does not seem much of a service to you, but as "our echoes go from soul to soul and go forever and forever," so the influence of this monument to the Aaronic Priesthood will also be going, we hope, as long as it stands, and the thoughts and principles belonging to it will go forever and forever.

# Four Marks of a Successful Missionary

*From an address given by President McKay at a missionary meeting in the Salt Lake Tabernacle held during general conference on April 3, 1959.*

I should like to name four things that each missionary should strive to be.

First, I would say he must be worthy of the call to represent the Lord and Savior Jesus Christ—the one perfect man who ever walked the earth, the source of the priesthood and power. Worthiness to represent him is essential.

Second, a testimony that he knows the gospel is the greatest thing in all the world; he senses it. We call it testimony; he is converted. A man must know what he teaches before he can bring others to it.

Third, a willingness to serve others, to go out of his way. Whenever one has something to do—something that he loves, something he is interested in—he wants somebody else to share that joy with him.

Fourth, inspiration, help, and seeking divine guidance through prayer. When one senses the glory of the gospel, when one realizes how comprehensive it is, what a great guide he has to a true philosophy of living; he senses his own need for help and guidance. Christ himself, perfect as he was, always sought his Father, particularly before any great event happened. When he fed the five thousand miraculously, God guided him to his own exercise of that power. Then he left on the Sabbath, spent the night in prayer, and told the disciples to cross the lake in the boat, that he would join them later. That was when the great miracle of walking on the water occurred. The disciples were surprised the next day to find him in Capernaum. Once a missionary senses that he can receive an answer and guidance, his difficulties will be overcome.

I pray God's blessings to enlarge each missionary's testimony and give him power to express appreciation of His love and guidance.

# Faith in the Gospel:
# Our Legacy to Youth

*From an address at the ninetieth semiannual general conference of the Church at an overflow meeting held in Barratt Hall October 5, 1919.*

I think nothing in this world can give such consolation, such peace, to fathers and mothers as to realize that their boys and girls have faith in the gospel of Jesus Christ. I may never be able to leave to my children wealth. Many of you may be unable to offer to your young sons, your young daughters, even a dollar to help them on their way. But I would rather live in poverty all the days of my life, I would rather be unable to give one cent to my boys and girls when they start out in life, if I were able, through sacrifice, diligent attention, and watchful care, to implant in their hearts a belief, a faith, in the gospel of Jesus Christ. I would rather do this than give them all the wealth and honor and distinction the powers of man may bestow. I *know* that a testimony of the gospel of Jesus Christ is the most sacred, the most precious gift in our lives.

Boys and girls, you cannot get that by following the paths of the world. You may get pleasure—momentary pleasure—by following the paths and the enticements of the world.

> *But pleasures are like poppies spread—*
> *You seize the flow'r, its bloom is shed;*
> *Or like the snow falls in the river—*
> *A moment white—then melts forever.*

A better definition of pleasure than this from the poet Robert Burns you cannot find in all literature! You may get that transitory pleasure, yes, but you cannot find joy; you cannot find happiness. Happiness is found only along that well-beaten track—narrow as it is, though straight—which leads to life eternal. That is my testimony to you. Sometimes there are obstacles. There is persecution; there is self-denial. There will be tears, because you are coming constantly in contact with these enticements, with these worldly ideals, and you have to overcome them, and for the moment there will seem to be sacrifice, but it is only temporary. The Lord never forsakes those who seek him. Never! I add my testimony to that which has been given. It may not come just the way you think but it will come. The Lord will certainly fulfill his promises to you.

# Courtesy and Self-Control in the Home

*From an address delivered by President McKay to the youth of the Church, from the Salt Lake Tabernacle, January 3, 1960. The final paragraph of this excerpt is taken from remarks by President McKay at the Sunday morning session of MIA June Conference June 14, 1959.*

Young people, marriage is a relationship that cannot survive selfishness, impatience, domineering, inequality, and lack of respect. Marriage is a relationship that thrives on acceptance, equality, sharing, giving, helping, doing one's part, learning, and laughing together.

Violation of the marriage vows proves the violator to be one who cannot be trusted, and "to be trusted is a greater compliment than to be loved."

Always keep in mind the fact that the covenant you make is a contributing factor to your happiness in marriage.

An important factor contributive to a happy marriage is self-control in the home. During courtship, keep your eyes wide open, but after marriage, keep them half shut. What I mean by this may be illustrated by the remark of a young woman who said to her husband, "I know my cooking isn't good. I hate it as much as you do; but do you find me sitting around griping about it?" This "griping" after marriage is what makes for unhappiness. A wise mate learns to control the tongue.

Do not speak the complaining word; just walk outdoors. I once heard of a couple who never had a quarrel, for they decided that whenever one lost his or her temper, he or she would go out and take a walk. He spent most of his time walking.

Another contributing factor is courtesy. During courtship each is pleased to anticipate the wishes of the other and, within the bounds of propriety, to take joy in granting those wishes. Too many couples look upon the covenant at the marriage altar as the end of courtship.

It should be the beginning of an eternal courtship, and that means the same consideration in the home for the wife that was given to her as a sweetheart in courtship; the same consideration for the husband, even though he sits behind the paper in the morning and doesn't say a word. Life becomes humdrum, but the humdrum is broken if we remember that "if you please," "thank you," and "pardon me" are just as appropriate and as much appreciated after marriage as before.

In the home blessed with children, children who see father courteous to mother and mother to father partake themselves of that attribute, just as they breathe the air of the home; and thus they become refined and cultured children, for the essence of true culture is consideration for others.

Do not forget—when difficulties arise, when debts begin to pile up and taxes have to be paid, when babies require coddling and perhaps feeding at night—that courtesy after marriage is a contributing factor toward harmony and peace in the home.

Nothing is more becoming in a great man than courtesy and forbearance. Be punctual with your wife and with your children. If duties detain you, do not hesitate to apologize and explain. Punctuality and consideration after marriage are important factors of a congenial home.

If you were to ask me what has contributed most to the happiness of my life and to the little success that I might have attained, I would say it was the master control exercised in our home by Sister McKay. Never a condition that could ruffle her character, no tardiness on my part (because of church meetings), never a hasty or impetuous answer or accusation—always a feeling of control over children, family, and all.

# My Mother

*Article printed in the* Instructor, *May, 1958.*

I cannot think of a womanly virtue that my mother did not possess. Undoubtedly, many a youth, in affectionate appreciation of his mother's love and unselfish devotion, can pay his mother the same tribute; but I say this in the maturity of manhood when calm judgment should weigh facts dispassionately. To her children, and all others who knew her well, she was beautiful and dignified. Though high spirited, she was even-tempered and self-possessed. Her dark brown eyes immediately expressed any rising emotion which, however, she had always held under perfect control.

In the management of her household she was frugal yet surprisingly generous, as was father also, in providing for the welfare and education of their children. To make home the most pleasant place in the world for her husband and children was her constant aim, which she achieved naturally and supremely. Though unselfishly devoted to her family, she tactfully taught each one to reciprocate in little acts of service.

Her soul, to quote the words of the poet, was, "As pure as lines of green that streak the first white of the snowdrop's inner leaves." In tenderness, watchful care, loving patience, loyalty to home and to right, she seemed to me in boyhood, and she seems to me now after these years, to have been supreme.

Mother left us when she was still young, only fifty-four. During the intervening years I have often wished that I had told her in my young manhood that my love for her and the realization of her love and of her confidence gave me power more than once during fiery youth to keep my name untarnished and my soul from clay.

From my beautiful, ever-devoted, and watchful mother, from my loyal sisters in our early home associations, and from my beloved wife during the maturer years that followed, I have received my high ideals of womanhood. No man has had inspiration from nobler, more loving women. To them I owe a debt of eternal gratitude.

Among my most precious soul treasures is the memory of mother's prayers by the bedside, of her affectionate touch as she tucked the bedclothes around my brother and me and gave each a loving, goodnight kiss. We were too young and roguish, then, fully to appreciate such devotion, but not too young to know that mother loved us.

It was this realization of mother's love, with a loyalty to the precepts of an exemplary father, which more than once during youth turned my steps from the precipice of temptation.

If I were asked to name the world's greatest need, I should say unhesitatingly *wise mothers*; and the second, *exemplary fathers*.

If mother love were but half rightly directed, and if fatherhood were but half what it should be in example and honor, much of the sorrow and wickedness in the world would indeed be overcome.

The home is the source of our national life. If we keep the spring pure, we shall have less difficulty in protecting the stream from pollution.

*My mother! God bless you!*
  *For your purity of soul,*
  *Your faith, your tenderness,*
  *Your watchful care,*
  *Your supreme patience,*
  *Your companionship and trust,*
  *Your loyalty to the right,*
  *Your help and inspiration to father,*
  *Your unselfish devotion to us children.*

# David O. McKay, A Great Teacher·

*From address delivered by President Stephen L Richards at the dedicatory services of the David O. McKay Building, Brigham Young University, Provo, Utah, December 14, 1954.*

Here is a teacher distinctive, set apart from other teachers of the world. One of his fundamental concepts in pedagogy is that there can be no adequate teaching of youth without personality, without making every truth and principle taught a motivating factor in the life and living of the individual. In his younger days he carried on his profession in the classroom and in the administration of a school. Through native endowment, industry, and study, he acquired great proficiency in the educational processes. Those who were in his classes, in his school, a half century ago remember him with great affection and gratitude, and their children have been told of the influence of his personality on the lives of their parents. But, after all, the lives of those touched immediately by his classroom work are relatively few in number. In young manhood he was called from his principalship of an academy to be a teacher in the kingdom of our Lord. He never deserted his profession. He expanded it. He dignified it, and he glorified it.

The Sunday Schools of the Church were the first beneficiaries of his art. He did much to bring order into their teaching. Uniform courses of study were established. The aims and objectives of lessons were clarified, and immeasurable inspiration was given to the teachers of this great organization for the application of gospel principles in making Latter-day Saints. The procedures fostered by him had influence in all the organizations of the Church. He brought untold improvement in their teaching procedure. His constant advocacy of personality as a potent factor in education has proved to be of inestimable value through the years. His attitude toward teaching has come about naturally from his abiding interest and faith in the individual. Every little boy or girl, and grown ones too, who has heard him speak to them has been made to feel that his or her individual welfare was the intimate concern of this great teacher. All who have come within the radiation of his teaching have been made to feel, not only that they have been enlightened by his exposition of truth, but also that they have a friend deeply concerned in their individual welfare.

*It would be impossible to list all of the splendid contributions of this great educator. Suffice it to say that five great institutions of learning recognized his high merits by granting him honorary degrees, and the whole church, with all its organizations, including particularly the department of*

*education, the colleges, schools, institutes and seminaries were all benefi-
ciaries of his outstanding accomplishments and contributions in the field of
education.—Clare Middlemiss*

# Index